OLD WEST PARANORMAL VOL. 2

TERROR ON THE TRAIN!

OLD WEST PARANORMAL VOL. 2

TERROR ON THE TRAIN!

Noe Torres & John LeMay

DEAD HORSE HISTORY

A SUBSIDIARY OF BICEP BOOKS, ROSWELL, NEW MEXICO

Printed in the United States of America

Torres, Noe and John LeMay.
Old West Paranormal Volume II: Terror on the Train!
ISBN 978-1-953221-13-1
Trains/Railroad/Paranormal

For my parents, who filled our home with books, and led me, as a child, to realize the power and importance of literature, as well as its beauty and ability to change a person's life forever.
—Noe Torres.

For my parents also, who bought me my first toy train set.
—John LeMay

A NOTE FROM THE AUTHOR

S ince 2011, my friend and co-author John LeMay and I have written a series of books about unexplained phenomena that happened during America's "Old West" period, roughly from the mid-1800s to the year 1900. We did exhaustive historical research, using the newspapers and other documents of the time, to uncover stories of unusual sightings of strange creatures, bizarre flying objects, futuristic contraptions, and many other events that remain unexplained even today.

While working on *The Real Cowboys & Aliens* series in particular, John and I found a number of newspaper stories and magazine articles featuring unexplained events involving trains and railroads that seemingly had a connection to UFOs or extraterrestrials. But we also found lots of bizarre railroad stories involving ghosts and other paranormal phenomena, rather than UFOs.

Thus, we decided to put together this little volume, in which we include many of these "other" strange, and possibly true, stories about trains, with more of an emphasis on ghosts and the paranormal, although a few UFO stories may have also snuck in!

Noe Torres

Edinburg, Texas
Oct. 23, 2024

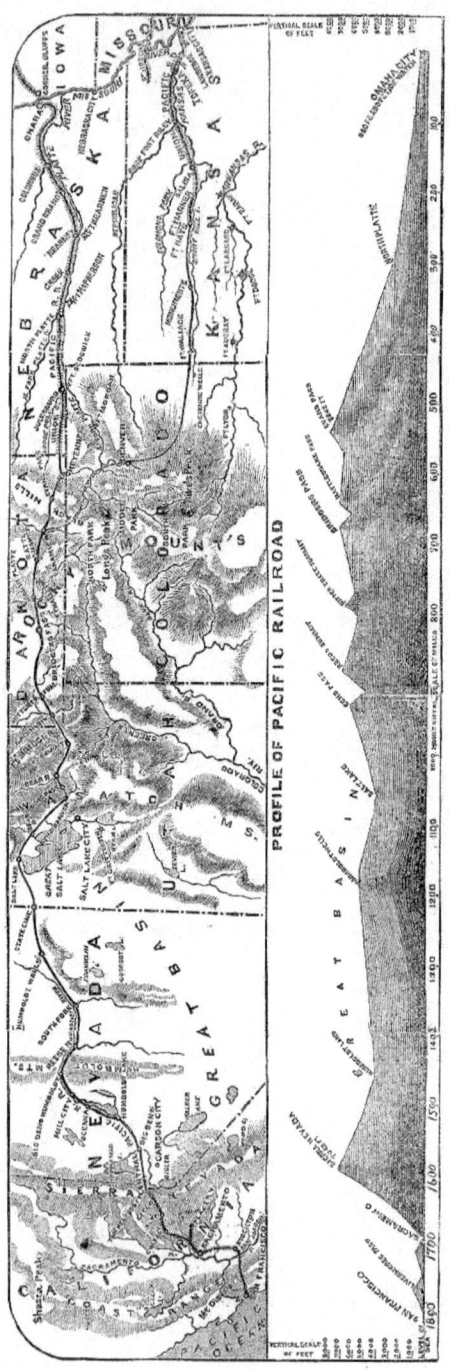

CENTRAL PACIFIC RAILROAD—MAP AND PROFILE MAP OF THE LINE FROM OMAHA TO SAN FRANCISCO.—[Drawn by C. H. Wells.]

TABLE OF CONTENTS

INTRODUCTION

A BRIEF HISTORY OF THE RAILROAD

I n our modern age of jet aircraft, outer space exploration, and world-wide computer networks, it is difficult to understand how important and revolutionary railroads were in North America in the late 19th century and early 20th century. Railroads made it possible for the United States to become what it is today, stretching from the Atlantic Ocean to the Pacific and from Canada to Mexico. The expansion of railroads made for efficient, if not speedy, movement of cargo and people from coast to coast.

The story of railroads in the United States began on July 4, 1828, with the construction of the Baltimore and Ohio Railroad (B&O), a 13-mile stretch connecting the port of Baltimore, Maryland, to the Ohio River. Although it seemed a modest beginning, the B&O was a significant milestone in the expansion of the U.S. rail network during the early 19th century.

The first transcontinental railroad network in the United States was completed on May 10, 1869, when the Union Pacific and Central Pacific railroads met at Promontory Summit, Utah, linking the eastern U.S. rail system with California. Within the next four decades, railroads connected most major cities and regions across the country, marking the completion of the extensive rail infrastructure that played a crucial role in the industrialization of the U.S. and the movement of goods and people.

The railroads inspired a significant cultural upheaval revolving around trains, train travel, and associated lore. From 1828 to 1919 and beyond, Americans became obsessed with trains. Both the journalism and the fiction of the time featured many stories about trains and events that happened aboard them. In 1843, one of America's earliest notable authors, Nathanial Hawthorne, wrote a story called "The Celestial Railroad," a satire about the industrial age's influence on spirituality and morality. Hawthorne argued that technological advancement did not necessarily equal moral advancement. Similarly, in American novelist Herman Melville's 1857 book *The Confidence-Man: His Masquerade* trains were given a prominent role as symbols of a new technology that would soon transform America.

Bret Harte, famous writer of Western stories, penned "The Outcasts of Poker Flats" in 1869, focusing on America's western expansion, especially via its new railroad infrastructure. Additionally, one of the first novels about mysterious happenings aboard a train was Arthur B. Reeve's *The Lost Express*, which mixed elements of crime and suspense to tell of a mysterious disappearance aboard a train. It was one of the first detective stories where trains were used to provide a claustrophobic and suspenseful environment for action and intrigue, which brings us to the theme of the book you now hold in your hands ....

Beginning in the late 1800s, stories about ghosts and other paranormal happenings aboard trains became extremely popular in America. "The Phantom Train of Marshall Pass," author unknown, told the story of a spectral train seen on the Denver and Rio Grande Railway. A ghostly train was seen speeding down the tracks at night, emitting no sound except for the faint echo of a whistle. The train was said to be a warning of impending disaster, and soon after sightings, accidents or derailments would occur. The haunting was believed to be connected to a tragedy where a train plunged off the Marshall Pass.

Another often-told story, "The Ghost Train of Bostian Bridge," concerned a ghostly train that was seen in the area near where a fatal train accident occurred on August 27 1891, in Statesville, North Carolina. A train plunged off Bostian Bridge, killing many passengers, and soon afterward, locals began reporting sightings of the ghostly train, along with eerie lights and the loud sounds of a crashing train. Witnesses claimed to hear the screams of passengers and the clatter of wreckage.

Yet another ghostly tale, "The Ghost Train of Lincoln, Nebraska," talked about people claiming to see a spectral locomotive moving down abandoned tracks late at night. This ghost train was said to travel silently, with passengers waving from the windows. Local people said the ghost train was haunted by the souls of railroad workers who had died on the job and were forever bound to the trains upon which they worked.

Perhaps the most influential of all such stories was "The Signal-Man," written in 1866 by Charles Dickens. Although Dickens was British, his story was widely read in America and inspired many American railroad ghost stories. In the tale, a signalman is haunted by ghostly warnings of train disasters. The story's eerie atmosphere, focused on the premonitions and hauntings of a railroad worker, was relatable to the American audience, especially since train accidents happened frequently in the 19th century.

However, the stories to follow in this book all fall into the category of non-fiction. And while we can't say whether they were true or not, the people who reported on these stories were, in fact, real. Were they telling tall tales with no truth at all, or did some of them actually happen? We will let you decide for yourself, so...listen to that distant, shrill moan of a train whistle approaching our location down a lonely stretch of long-abandoned railroad tracks. And, can you hear those screams and the sounds of crashing, grinding metal? But there are no trains anywhere in sight; nor have there been trains running through here in decades! With this thought in mind, you are now well prepared for the strange stories that lurk in the pages ahead.

YARNS BY A TRAIN'S CREW.

QUEER STORIES THAT WERE TOLD IN A FLYING BAGGAGE CAR.

Engineers Haunted by Mishaps—A Spectral Funeral Train Celebrating an Anniversary—Cars Thrown Over Telegraph Poles.

Then there was narrated a weird story that I had heard once before. It was about an apparition of a train on the Hudson River Railroad. It was told with an effort at sincerity that did not deceive the listener, but I am told that there are many trackmen and laborers along the line of the Hudson River Railroad who pretend to have seen the spectacle. The tale was about a mystic counterpart of the funeral train that bore Abraham Lincoln's remains from this city to the West. The actual and substantial train passed over the road on a certain day in April, 1865. The car that contained the President's remains was heavily draped I believe. It is said that on that night, every year, all the train men who are on the road during a certain hour (that varies in different subdivisions of the road) hear and see and feel the spectre train rush by them. It sounds hollow and awful. Its lights are yellow, pale, and funereal. Its train hands and passengers are sepulchral figures. It looks like the outline of a train, yet every detail is perfect. Those who have seen it say, though they felt that it was only a vision, that a man could walk through it if he dared, or throw a stone through it; yet it seems perfect in everything but substantialness. It even carries with it a whirl of wind as fast trains do, but it is a cold, clammy, gravelike atmosphere, all its own. As it passes another train the shriek of its whistle and clang of its bell strike terror to the hearts of those that hear them.

The New York Sun of July 29, 1879, p.4.

1

LINCOLN'S GHOSTLY FUNERAL TRAIN

1879
NEW YORK

Following a sensational national tragedy, collectively experienced by all citizens, it seems that reports of paranormal activity increase dramatically. This was certainly the case following the very first assassination of an American president – Abraham Lincoln on April 15, 1865. The "ghost" of Lincoln has been seen on numerous occasions, especially in and around the White House. Following his death, a shocked nation tried to make sense of what had occurred, even as a grateful federal government carried out a series of memorial events to commemorate Lincoln's outstanding accomplishments as president.

It was decided that Lincoln's body should be taken by train along the 1,564-mile trek from Washington, D.C. to his hometown of Springfield, Illinois, with stops along the way. Thus, on April 21, 1865, an ornate, nine-car funeral train departed Washington, pulled by a steam locomotive carrying a framed portrait of Lincoln and a wreath on the front. The nine cars of the train were draped in black bunting and included a car for the hearse and horses, the president's car, as well as accommodations for the entourage that would accompany the bodies of Lincoln and his son William Wallace Lincoln, who had died of typhoid at age 11 in 1862.

The Lincoln Funeral Locomotive. (Wikimedia)

The funeral train passed through 180 cities in seven states, taking a route designed to pass through most major cities in the Northeast, including a stop in New York City on April 24, during which Lincoln's casket was removed from the train and paraded through the city.

Lincoln's Funeral Procession in New York City.
(Library of Congress)

Terror on the Train!

Continuing on from New York City, the funeral train proceeded along the Hudson Valley, headed toward Illinois, travelling mostly at night. At many stations along the way, spectators caught a glimpse of the eerie procession of train cars shrouded in darkness passing solemnly through their town. This strange, surreal sight probably contributed to future sightings of a ghostly funeral train, seen many years after 1865.

For example, in a *New York Sun* article published 14 years after Lincoln's funeral procession (July 29, 1879), witnesses told a bizarre story about the apparition of a "specter train" every year on the Hudson River Railroad. Occurring on the annual anniversary of the 1865 passing of Lincoln's funeral train, the spooky manifestation was reportedly seen by "many trackmen and laborers along the line of the Hudson River Railroad."

"It is said that on that night, every year, all the train men that are on the road at a certain hour (that varies in various subdivisions of the road), hear and see and feel the specter train rush by them. It sounds hollow and awful. Its lights are yellow, pale and funereal. Its train hands and passengers are sepulchral figures. It looks like the outline of a train, yet every detail is perfect."

The *New York Sun* article continued, "Those who have seen it say, though they felt that it was only a vision, that a man could walk through it if he dared, or throw a stone through it; yet it seems perfect in everything but substantialness. It even carries with it a whirl of wind as fast as trains do, but it is a cold, clammy, grave-like atmosphere, all its own. As it passes another train the shriek of its whistle and clang of its bell strike terror to the hearts of those that hear them."

Historical Marker. (Courtesy Pomeroy Foundation).

Other sightings of a spectral version of Lincoln's funeral train have been reported over the years. In the town of Hyde Park, New York, the local historical society said this on their web site, "Shortly before 8pm on April 25 [1865], the president's funeral train passed through the town of Hyde Park. Ever since this momentous occasion, a story has been told of an eerie event that occurs along the tracks in Hyde Park each night on April 25. If the moon is out, clouds are said to obscure it. A black carpet seems to roll down the tracks and deadens all sound. Then, Lincoln's funeral train, adorned in black crepe is seen slowing inching its way north to Albany. This is not the only story told of sightings of the ghost of Lincoln's funeral train. One will hear of similar stories that have been passed along in communities located along the train's path that still resonate with locals to this day."

The Lincoln Funeral car.

Just north of Hyde Park is Albany, where the eerie ghostly train has also been spotted over the years. This account comes from the *Albany Evening Times*: "The train always appeared in Albany on...the anniversary of its first passing. Track walkers and section hands would sit along the railroad tracks in the early evening of the fateful day and wait for the ghost train to come into view. At midnight - always at midnight - the engine would emerge from the darkness, moving silently down the track with black crepe flowing from its sides, emitting faintly audible funeral music..."

Ghostly train sightings have been reported all along the route from Washington, D.C. to Illinois. In Chicago, where Lincoln's funeral train passed on the way to Springfield back in 1865, there have also been ghostly sightings of a spectral train.

Scientists and psychologists say these sightings were a result of the deep sense of shock and mourning that befell the United States following the sudden killing of its beloved president. But, perhaps it was just what the witnesses said it was -- a ghost train.

2

GHOST TRAIN OF MARSHALL PASS

LATE 1800s
ROCKY MOUNTAINS, COLORADO

In 1889, a number of Western newspapers, citing the *Denver News* as the source, published a story about a "phantom train" seen by many train crews at Marshall Pass in the Rocky Mountains, located at 10,842 feet elevation. It was reported that crews of the Denver & Rio Grande Railroad Company saw this ghost train frequently, sometimes as often as three times a day, with "ghostly forms" peering out its windows.

For the crews operating the trains at such high elevations and in such a rugged, mountainous landscape, danger was a constant companion. However, these railroad men were of a "fearless class," according to the *Denver Times*. "Journeys of so perilous a nature that the blood of an ordinary man would curdle at the bare thought of one undertaken, are successfully made by them, and under circumstances of so trying a character that, on reflection, the average man would marvel at."

And yet, many of these otherwise unflappable railroad workers expressed no eagerness toward operating a train over the Marshall Pass. The *Times* spoke to one veteran train engineer who when asked about the pass, "he involuntarily [clinched] his hands and pales visibly" and replied that he "would not pull a train over Marshall Pass for a cool million." It was known that train engineers tended to be extremely cautious in the area of the pass, where they "usually hugged the rail there as close as possible."

Most of the engineers who complained about seeing the phantom train were those that pulled the night passenger train from Salida, Colorado, which reached Green River at 7 a.m. In addition to complaining, many of them subsequently quit their jobs.

After another engineer on the nighttime passenger run quit, the company brought in an "old-and-tried" engineer named Nelson Edwards and his fireman, Charles Whitehead. "Both men were cool and calculating, well-educated and generally considered the most fearless men in the employ of the Rio Grande – men who had caught runaway trains in the mountain side without so much as a flush suffusing their cheeks."

Denver & Rio Grande Railroad train at Marshall Pass, circa 1890.

Edwards and Whitehead operated the nighttime passenger run across the Marshall Pass for several months without incident. "For nearly two months, they were on the train, back and forth every other day, and while the alternating crews had changed several times, they had not seen the mysterious train, the sight of which had been the cause of so many engineers quitting that division."

And then one night, Engineer Edwards felt unusually tense and uneasy. He had heard reports that one of the bridges up ahead might be in danger of falling down and also that there might be a defective rail in one of the canyons. While trying to focus especially hard on his job, Edwards suddenly heard a deeply concerning sound – long warning whistles from another train coming up from behind them and closing.

"Again, when about five miles further on, he recognized the same whistle, this time nearer, and at short intervals the signal was heard, coming rapidly nearer. It must be a wild train, Whitehead grumbled, as the engineer reached for the rope and gave two short, sharp whistles, only to hear the long, dangerous answer."

At one point, the train was temporarily stopped but then continued moving forward. "The train increased in momentum as it moved forward, and in about five minutes was running as fast as practicable on that portion of the road. The following train was approaching nearer and nearer. Again, the short series of warning whistles was heard, which Edwards answered, but only to hear the wild train give the danger signal again."

Edwards looked out of the window as he was rounding a curve and noticed the other train approaching. "Cold beads of sweat stood out on his forehead as he pulled the throttle wide open. Faster and faster the speed of the train increased, and more dangerous was the track. They were now in the very worst portion of the pass, where the snowbanks were the most treacherous, and just in this part of the track was where the broken rail was reported."

"The cars were rocking violently. The train was lurching frightfully. The passengers were rudely awakened from their slumbers by the train striking a snowdrift. The speed of the train was so great that the train broke the drift easily and was soon soaring through a snow shed. How the fireman labored -- his shirt was wet with perspiration, for the hungry furnace consumed the coal so quickly that the stack belched fire. The

23

passengers having been warned of the impending danger, had dressed themselves. The women were wringing their hands in despair, strong men were trembling...."

"At this time the snow began to descend, and in the peculiar light that settles on the earth, caused by the snow, Edwards saw something in a backward glance he took that made his blood freeze, and almost caused his heart to cease beating. On the top of one of the cars of the rear train was a tall white figure of a man gesticulating wildly, while he could see a white form in the cab."

Now about 200 yards ahead of the other train, Edwards eased the train into a spot where the track reversed and ran parallel. The maneuver brought him momentarily side-by-side with the mystery train.

"As he passed the other engine, he saw two extremely white figures in the cab. The specter engineer turned face to him like so, and laughed. The ghostly fireman reached for the cord, and again a series of short, sharp whistles sounded. On the train plunged into the night, roaring through snowsheds and over iron bridges that trembled beneath the sudden shock. So fast was the train traveling that the rush of air could be heard by the passengers."

Marshall Pass in 1899. (Library of Congress)

Once again in the lead, Edwards powered up his train to the highest speed it could go. The phantom train was still gaining. "The greatest speed his engine was capable of had been attained, and Edwards could but watch the rail in front of him and keep his hand on the throttle. The phantom train was gaining; he could go no faster; he was helpless. Around the shelves of high mountains and along the ridge of lofty hills, over deep arroyos, through long snow sheds the race continued: the very landscape was closing behind the train like a cloud; the mountains seemed to recede rapidly, but all the while the specter train was gaining ground."

After a while, Edwards noticed what looked like a crew of railway workers that seemed to be working on the tracks. Upon closer examination, it was clear they were not human. "Far ahead he observed light, shadowy, fantastic forms, and as the train drew nearer, he saw that they were repairing the track. They were spirits, and the next minute, flying toward the ghosts on the track, passed through the crowd of ten or twelve, reached the curve beyond, and Edwards ventured a backward glance."

And then, the mysterious train that had pursued so closely for so many miles suddenly skidded off the tracks and flew down the embankment, as if to its doom. "He [Edwards] saw the phantom train run to a broken rail, the engine ran off onto the ties, and one second later the heavy freight pitched down the embankment and a moment later vanished. Written in the frost of the fireman's window was the following message with very poor spelling and grammar, written in a very peculiar hand:

> "Yoers ago a frate train was recked as yu saw—now that yu saw it, we will never make another run. The enjine was not ounder cantrol, and four sexshun men wor killed. If yu ever run on this road again yu will be recked."

Finally rid of his pursuer, Edwards traveled onward toward Green River, Colorado, which he reached at 6.am., an hour ahead of schedule. Later in the day, Edwards quit his job with the Denver & Rio Grande Railroad and later got a job with the Union Pacific Railroad, where he was considered "one of the most trustworthy men in their employ."

Among the many newspapers that ran this story was the May 18, 1889 edition of the *St. Louis (Missouri) Globe-Democrat*, which we used for this chapter. All of the newspapers gave the primary source of the story as the *Denver Times* newspaper. (The *Denver Times* was a daily newspaper in Denver, Colorado, during 1872 to 1926. It was merged into the *Rocky Mountain News* in 1926.)

3

THE PHANTOM TRAIN

The Old West was replete with stories about spectral trains that would suddenly appear along lonely stretches of tracks or even where railroad lines were long abandoned or nonexistent. A ghostly train whistle would be followed by the loud noise of an oncoming locomotive, and then terrified spectators would see a shimmering, translucent train go streaking past, often vanishing into thin air right before their eyes.

In this chapter, we will examine one particular case that is often included with "ghost train" stories, but was actually not a ghost train sighting at all. Rather, it seems to have been a sighting of another one of the mysterious futuristic air or land vehicles that occasionally turned up in North America in the 1800s.

This story, first appearing in the *Kansas City (Kansas) Pioneer* on August 1, 1878, has a number of very unique characteristics that make it worth further study. Unlike typical ghost train encounters, this case took place in broad daylight. Twelve witnesses observed a strange craft that definitely did not look like a train travelling along the railroad tracks before it suddenly veered off the tracks and plowed through thickly-forested woods.

With the headline "A Phantom Train Tearing Down on the K. P. Road at Edwardsville," the newspaper article reported,

"Edwardsville is twelve miles west of Kansas City, on the Kansas Pacific Road, and has a haunted house, and has been the theater of many mysterious sights and sounds. But the following, which occurred in daylight, and to which there were a dozen eyewitnesses, is one of the most remarkable occurrences on record. Mr. Timmons, our informant, is one of the most substantial farmers and reliable men in Wyandotte County."

A search of historical records shows that J. F. Timmons was an influential landowner, farmer, and member of the political party known as the Greenbacks. According to *Wikipedia*, "The Greenback Party was an American political party with an anti-monopoly ideology which was active between 1874 and 1889.

The party ran candidates in three presidential elections -- in the elections of 1876, 1880, and 1884, before fading away."

Timmons told the newspaper, "Last Tuesday morning [July 30], the section men on the Kansas Pacific Road on my farm, seeing the storm coming up on the track, got their handcar and started full speed for Edwardsville. They had run but a little way, when the entire crowd at the same time, saw coming around the curve east of Edwardsville, what they supposed to be a locomotive at full speed."

Railroad Crew with Handcar, Ca. 1921

These "section men" were apparently doing routine maintenance on the tracks using a handcar when they became aware of what seemed to be a storm, or some kind of atmospheric disturbance, off in the distance. They got into their handcar and began heading toward the nearby town of Edwardsville. Suddenly, they heard what sounded like a locomotive coming toward them at full speed, raising the specter of a head-on crash.

Timmons continued, "They jumped down and took their car off the track as fast as possible, when they saw that it was not a locomotive. Whatever it was, it came down the track, giving off a volume of dense smoke with occasional flashes resembling a headlight in the center of the smoke." Although this story is often included with other stories about "ghost trains," it was clearly not a train. The eyewitnesses said that although it "sounded" like a train, it was definitely "not a locomotive."

Timmons continued, "It came three-fourths of a mile from where they first saw it, then turned off the track at a pile of cordwood, went round it once, then went in a southwesterly direction through a thick wood. The section men came running to my house, evidently much frightened and bewildered by what they saw. What was it?"

A PHANTOM TRAIN

Tearing Down on the K. P. Road, at Edwardsville,

FRIGHTENS THE SECTION MEN AND CAUSES THEM TO CLEAR THE TRACK.

It Frisks Off Around a Wood-Pile, and Disappears in the Forest, Amid Fire and Smoke.

Edwardsville is twelve miles west of Kansas City, on the K. P. road, and has a haunted house, and has been the theater of many mysterious sights and sounds. But the following which occurred in daylight, and to which there are a dozen eye witnesses, is one of the most remarkable occurences on record Mr. Timmons, our informant is one of the most substantial farmers and reliable men in Wyandott county.

Edwardsville, July 31, 1878. — Last Teusday morning, the section men on the K. P. road on my farm, seeing the storm coming up very fast, got their hand car on the track and started full speed for Edwardsville. They had run but a little ways when the entire crowd at the same time, saw coming around the curve east of Edwardsville, what they supposed to be a locomotive at full speed, they jumped down and took their car off the track as fast as possible, when they saw it was not a locomotive. Whatever it was came down the track giving off a volume of dense smoke with occasional flashes resembling a head light in the center of the smoke. It came three-fourths of a mile from where they first saw it, then, turned off the track at a pile of cord wood, went around it once, then went off in a south westerly direction, through a thick wood. The section men came running to my house evidently much frightened, and bewildered by what they saw. What was it?
J. F. TIMMONS.

The Weekly Pioneer (Kansas City, Kansas), 8-1-1878, p.4

Bearing a striking similarity to the fictional time machine locomotive from the motion picture *Back to the Future III*, this strange vehicle spotted in 1878 remains totally unexplained even today. That it was not actually a train is very clear and that it did not require tracks upon which to move is also certain.

Also interesting is that its appearance was immediately preceded by an atmospheric disturbance, perhaps the opening of a portal or wormhole, through which the strange vehicle traveled. Could it have been another instance of an object from the future or from another dimension intruding upon the unsuspecting denizens of the 19th century? Or, might it have been extraterrestrial in origin, having first landed from the sky and then moved along the most convenient "roadway," which would have been the railroad tracks?

1819 built locomotive. (Library of Congress)

The newspaper account points out the uniqueness of this case, said that the incident "which occurred in daylight, and to which there are a dozen eye-witnesses, is one of the most remarkable occurrences on record." Given the unique nature of the sighting, the event does not really lend itself to being grouped with other "phantom train" tales, which generally happened at night and were seen by only one or two witnesses.

This wasn't the only "otherworldly" train encounter that the authors dug up, though. There was another in which a glowing fireball came streaking out of the sky and slammed into a moving train! The story "The Locomotive Met a Ball of Fire," was published in the June 11, 1891 edition of the *Binghamton [New York] Herald*. The article said, "An engineer on the Delaware, Lackawanna and Western says he was coming down the Chenango valley when the recent storm burst. A vivid flash of lightning startled him, but he was not prepared for what followed. A huge ball of fire was seen on one of the rails coming rapidly toward the locomotive. He shut off steam and reversed the engine. The lightning, which looked like a ball of liquid fire about the size of a twelve-inch football, struck the driving wheels of the locomotive and, after running several times around them, crossed over on the axles to the opposite side of the track and went spinning away in the direction from which it came and vanished around a distant curve. The engine was not damaged, with the exception of the glass oilers on the side rods, which were broken, and the paint on the 'driver' was blistered."

The fact that the paint was blistered is interesting and offered proof that the train had in fact come into contact with something highly unusual. Was the 12-inch fireball that struck the train some kind of energy beam fired from a UFO? Or perhaps it was an unmanned probe of some type that was speeding down the tracks on an unknown mission before colliding with the locomotive?

4

PHANTOMS OF
DOVE CREEK

1869-PRESENT
KELTON, UTAH

One of the most historic spots in the history of the railroad is that of the Sinks of Dove Creek, a former railroad camp near Kelton, Utah, and the Golden Spike National Historic Site. It was there in May of 1869 that the Transcontinental Railroad was officially completed. To commemorate the occasion, golden spikes were pounded into a laurel tie with silver-headed sledgehammers by dignitaries from the Union and Central Pacific railroads alike.

In Earl Murray's book, *Ghosts of the Old West*, in the chapter entitled "Night of the Iron Horse," the author told of the spectral train sightings of Steve Ellison in that same area. Ellison was both a historian and park ranger at the time he had his sightings at the location of the Sinks of Dove Creek in September 1979.

It just so happened that Ellison and some friends were marching up the old Central Pacific Railroad route as part of a historical reenactment. All of the members were dressed in authentic army uniforms (including .45–70 Springfield rifles) of the time which were similar to those of the 21st infantry which were assigned to protect the workers back in the late 1860s. Upon reaching the Sinks of Dove Creek, they set up their tents for the night. To keep things as authentic as possible, certain members of the reenactment actually stood guard for the night. Ellison recalled having guard duty sometime past midnight just above the encampment. The summer had stretched into September and so it was still unusually warm even at night, he remembered. Ellison recalled that there was no moon that night, but the stars were bright enough that he had a good range of vision in the darkness. When Ellison looked down at his encampment, he could see the campfires of friends flickering in between the rows of tents.

Ceremony for the driving of the golden spike at Promontory Summit, Utah, on May 10, 1869.

Suddenly, a sound that reminded him of "the muffled roar of a rocket" broke the silence. His head darted in the direction of the noise and he saw a small light in the distance that looked as though it was swinging from side to side. All the while the muffled roar morphed into the noise of a *chug-chug-chug-chug*, increasing in intensity as it drew nearer. He stood there rooted to the spot as though he was unable to move. The light had disappeared and now it was only the strange noise of what could only be an invisible train. "Then the sound seemed to rush up over me in a kind of blast, soaring right over my head," Ellison said in *Ghosts of the Old West*. It terrified Ellison to the point that his knees were shaking.

Terror on the Train!

Ellison ran back to camp, sticking near the fire in front of his tent, his body still trembling and shaking. Ellison fought the urge to wake up the other guard, as he still had several hours of sleep designated. Ellison gathered his nerve and decided to return to his post. As he walked the path, he then heard the noises of footsteps and whispering. Although part of him wanted to dash back to camp, he gathered his resolve and listened. To his shock, the whispers he heard appeared to be in Chinese, which made sense whereas ghosts were concerned since many of the laborers of the Sinks of Dove Creek had been Chinese immigrants.

Sinks of Dove Creek. (BLM photo)

Though the circumstances were certainly strange, Ellison realized he was in no danger, and decided to simply observe what was happening. As he let himself relax, he became aware of more voices and noises, such as the bustling of men at work along the railroad. One noise in particular he decided must have been spikes being hammered into the rails. Although he couldn't see the men themselves, when he looked at the old railroad tracks, he could see little pinpricks of light and sparks flying from the rails as if the invisible ghosts were pounding at them.

The next morning, Ellison reluctantly told his friends of the encounter. He had been frightened that they would not believe him, but instead they were disappointed that he didn't wake them to see it for themselves. Later Ellison would learn that the old Pacific grade where he had his sighting has had many paranormal events over the years including what he experienced, which seemed to be the sound of a ghost train riding along invisible rails. In fact, that was why so many people avoided that portion of the railroad which remained in a state of disrepair. People were afraid that the ghost train might actually run them over. As it turned out, engineers told stories in private of phantom trains rushing at them through the desert and nearly overtaking them.

In reflecting on the incident, author Earl Murray put forth the notion that perhaps Ellison had walked through a time window, crossing dimensions into the past for just a moment. Of the incident, Murray wrote on page 110, "Some feel that an impression in time exist there, or that perhaps lost spirits of dead laborers have returned to fill the energy they created in building the railroad. Whatever it is, something is there."

5

ALIEN ABDUCTION FROM TRAIN?

MAY 1911
PIQUA, OHIO

Though alien abductions have possibly been occurring since the dawn of time, the idea of alien abduction didn't truly seep into the public consciousness until the Betty and Barney Hill case of 1961. This was the first instance to include the major characteristics of what we now consider a typical abduction, including missing time, strange creatures, and bodily evidence that the witnesses had been through some sort of physical ordeal.

While driving in New Hampshire's White Mountains on the night of September 19, 1961, the Hills saw a bright light in the sky that seemed to be pursuing them. It turned out to be an oddly shaped, 40-foot-long UFO with flashing, multicolored lights. Both Betty and Barney Hill "blacked out" and experienced "missing time." It was only later, while under hypnosis, that they both described being taken aboard the UFO, where a series of apparent medical examinations were conducted on them by a group of strange humanoid creatures. The two abductees were haunted by their experience, suffering from nightmares and other problems for many years after their encounter.

In recent years, researchers have begun to see a correlation between abductees and post-traumatic stress disorder. Some abductees find the memories of their abductions so disturbing that they sometimes develop psychological problems. Some will even commit suicide for fear of being abducted again.

Dr. J. Allen Hynek

In late November of 1973, world-famous astronomer and UFO researcher J. Allen Hynek received a letter from a 77-year-old named Elsie Fox Shirley who described the traumatic experience of an abductee that predated the Betty and Barney Hill case by exactly 50 years.

The incident happened to Shirley's sister, Idella Fox Ford (1876-1913), in 1911. At the time, Idella was a 36-year-old music teacher and mother of two sons – Bernard, 12, and Floyd, 10. She lived just outside of Piqua, Ohio, in Union County. She was divorced from Dr. Carl Ford, of Broadway, Ohio, a physician and preacher, whom she married in 1898.

In mid-May 1911, Idella boarded a train to go visit her grandmother, who lived 40 miles away in Broadway. Conveniently, her grandmother actually lived across the street from the railroad depot, so Idella could simply walk there when she arrived.

In a shocking turn of events, after arriving in Broadway, Idella stumbled into her grandmother's home in a state of extreme emotional and physical duress. Although many years would pass before she finally revealed what happened to her, she eventual told family members that "they" had come from the sky to take her, and she lived the rest of her life in fear of these mysterious beings that might someday come back and "take" not only her, but other members of her family also. More specifically, she was terribly frightened that the beings would "destroy" her and her family.

In addition to the bizarre account of beings from the sky, Idella also had strange marks on her body that apparently resulted from her "abduction," if that is what it was. First, something very hot had seared her face, and her tongue was strangely swollen. On her calves were three indentations that seemed to have been made by a hand with only three fingers. Interestingly, grey aliens are often depicted with only three fingers and one thumb on each hand.

This was the secret that finally came out after many years of a strange silence. Right after the incident happened, Idella was so distraught that her grandmother called Idella's mother, Mrs. Ida Fox, to come at once. Ida, and her son, raced to Broadway from Delaware, Ohio, 14 miles away, as quickly as they could by horse and buggy.

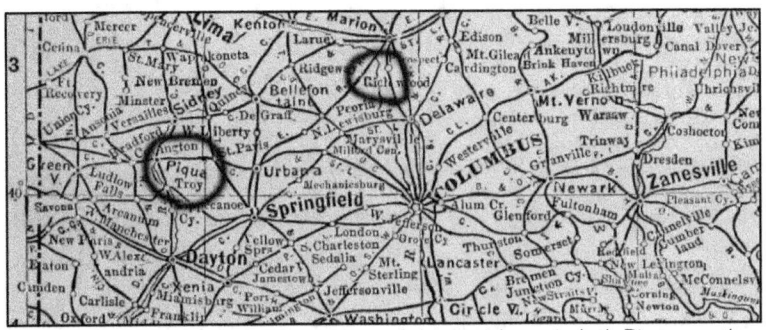

1911 Ohio map with the key areas of this incident circled, Piqua on the left and Broadway on the right.

At the same time, one of Idella's other brothers travelled to Idella's home to look in on her two boys. He asked them if their mother had seemed upset when she left, but they said she seemed fine and happy when she boarded the train. What exactly happened to Idella during her voyage was a great mystery for many years, with Idella offering few clues and only rarely providing minor hints about her ordeal.

Many people tried to get Idella to talk about the experience. When asked, Idella would become so upset as to become incoherent. Several doctors examined her, one of which was her brother, D.C. Fox, and all agreed that something unusual had happened to her. The physical manifestations of her ordeal were clearly present on her body, and her overall behavior had changed dramatically since the incident.

When she finally disclosed her story, she did so only to her mother and her sister Elsie, who years later sent a letter to J. Allen Hynek about her sister's abduction.

Mrs. Idella Ford Attempts Suicide.

Word was received at Broadway, Tuesday, that Mrs. Idella Ford, a former resident of that village, had attempted suicide by throwing herself in the Scioto river, near Radnor, Delaware county. She was rescued in time to save her life

Mrs. Ford is a daughter of Mrs. Ida L. Fox, who lives on the old Coben place, near Radnor. The daughter has been living in Piqua for several years, where she conducted a boarding house. She came to the home of her mother on a visit the first of the week, and her mind is thought to be unbalanced by domestic troubles which have extended over a period of several years.

Marysville (OH) Journal-Tribune, Nov. 26, 1912, p. 3

Sadly, Idella's life did not have a happy ending. After the ordeal, she and her sons moved in with her mother, and Idella lapsed into a suicidal frame of mind. On one occasion, the family stopped her from jumping off a high beam located in a barn. Another time, she was rescued from trying to drown herself in the nearby Scioto River.

With the concept of alien visitation and abduction being totally unknown in 1911, Idella's mother concluded that her daughter was insane and had her committed to the Columbus State Mental Hospital in Columbus, Ohio. After committing Idella, Mrs. Fox burned Idella's journal, in which she gave details about her bizarre encounter. Mrs. Fox felt that the journal entries were simply the ramblings of a mentally disturbed person and destroyed them all.

On October 13, 1913, after being at the state hospital for exactly 10 months, Idella hanged herself in her hospital room. As reported in the local newspapers she tore pieces from her bedsheet and fastened the cloth to the top horizontal metal bar covering her window. A report in the *Richwood (Ohio) Gazette* said, "Standing for several hours with her face pressed against one of the windows of the Columbus State hospital, Mrs. Idella Ford, a suicide, was seen by many patients and attendants Monday. Not knowing, however, that the woman was dead, no particular attention was paid to the fact that she stood in the window apparently looking out. About four o'clock Monday afternoon, considering the action of the patient to be unusual, an investigation was made, and the attendants were greatly shocked at finding a corpse in the window."

The article continued, "It is presumed that Mrs. Ford hanged herself quite early in the morning. She had tied a sheet about her neck, fastening one end to the iron bar at the top of the window in her room. When found, the tips of her toes were resting on the window sill."

The *Gazette* added a statement suggesting that Idella had been driven to madness by a recent illness, along with the trauma of her divorce. "Some time ago, the suicide passed through a siege of typhoid fever, and her illness, together with worry over her marital trouble, unbalanced her mind." Although the article mentions a previous suicide attempt, it does not discuss the strange encounter that happened to Idella in 1911.

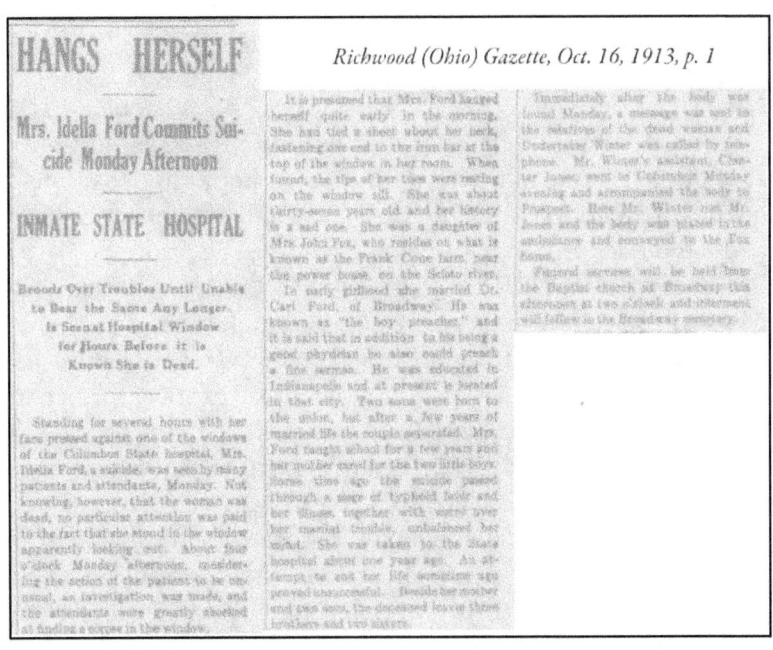

Richwood (Ohio) Gazette, Oct. 16, 1913, p. 1

In fact, no mention is made of her strange encounter in any of the notices published about her death. Her "abduction" story was clearly considered to be just the ravings of a deranged person. Interestingly, the account of her death given in The *Marion (Ohio) Star* on October 15, 1913, gives an alternate possible cause for her mental problems. The *Star* said, "Brooding over religious matters brought about her mental derangement." What "religious matters" would these have been? Is it possible that people overheard her talking about beings that came from the sky and "took" her, as well as her fears that these "sky beings" would come back and destroy her and her family? To someone unfamiliar with the context of what happened to Idella, it might sound like religious, apocalyptic visions.

Decades later, when Elsie learned about UFOs and alien abductions, she finally pieced together in her mind what might have really happened to Idella – that she had somehow been abducted back in 1911, and consequently, she wrote her letter to Dr. Hynek in 1973. This very sad and tragic story seems far too realistic to be dismissed as a fabrication. Significantly, we have been able to use the historical records to verify all of the information about the persons involved and most of the events mentioned by Elsie in her letter to Hynek.

But truthfully, could Idella have been abducted from a moving train? There have certainly been stranger tales of abduction. Some abductees have reported being taken from moving automobiles and from rooms with locked doors and no windows. If not from a moving train, perhaps Idella was taken during one of the rest stops along the train route between her home and her destination.

6

GHOSTLY FORM APPEARS ON TRAIN

NOVEMBER 1885
PROVIDENCE, RHODE ISLAND

S tories of phantoms appearing on or near trains usually surfaced after a railroad tragedy had occurred in the same area in the years prior to the apparition. Typically, the phantom was said to be an unfortunate soul that had lost his life in the earlier tragedy and was now cursed to appear at the scene of the accident – apparently to warn others of "danger ahead."

In November 1885, a ghostly apparition was seen near Providence, Rhode Island, onboard a newly-rebuilt steam engine locomotive called the *Matt Morgan*. The engine had been rebuilt because it was involved in a horrific accident ten years earlier, in November 1875.

The *Matt Morgan*, which had exploded back in 1875 and killed its engineer, was rebuilt slowly over time and put back into service almost exactly ten years later. Although there was reportedly a great reluctance among engineers to work on the *Matt Morgan*, an engineer was finally found. The local newspaper said, "When the engine which made the terrible leap on that stormy night was rebuilt and put on the road again, there was at first great trouble in getting engineers for it, with such a superstitious horror was it regarded."

On its very first trip in its new incarnation, the engine was once again approaching the city of Providence when something very unusual happened, according to the locomotive engineer.

The November 19, 1885 edition of the *New York Democrat and Chronicle* reported, "On the first trip that she made after being rebuilt she went tearing into Providence in the night with the swinging behind and the sleeping town echoing to the shrill whistle. On approaching the station, the engineer leaned forward to shut off the steam, but to his horror a ghostly form appeared at his side and a ghostly hand grasped his wrist and held him fast."

The terrified engineer felt his hand in an iron grip that prevented him from shutting the engine down in time to bring the train to a stop at the Providence station. Try as he might, he was unable to fight off the ghostly hand that kept him from working the engine's controls.

Immediately after the train passed the Providence train station, the ghostly apparition vanished, and the engineer regained control of the vessel, bringing it to a stop some distance beyond the Providence station.

Typical American Steam Locomotive, circa 1890.

After the frightened engineer reported what had happened to him, he was reminded of the horrible accident that claimed the life of the previous engineer of the *Matt Morgan* in November 1875. It was suggested to him that the ghostly form he saw on the train was, in fact, the spirit of the dead engineer that had appeared to possibly try to prevent another disaster.

The *Democrat and Chronicle* said, "Many people have not forgotten the terrible Richmond switch disaster several years ago on the Providence and Stonington Road." The dead engineer was known for always giving two "peculiar whistles" as he approached Providence in order to alert his wife, who lived near the railroad, that he was alright and would soon be home. After the accident, it was said that local people heard the unusual train whistles in the area, even when no trains were anywhere around. The newspaper said, "Today there are people ready to swear that they have heard whistles, such as [the engineer] used to blow as signals to his wife, sound through the suburbs of Providence, when no train was coming up the road."

After the reported ghostly encounter, reporters scrambled to find information about the 1875 accident that caused the death of the *Matt Morgan* engineer, William Fiske, as well as a second worker, John Knowles. According to an article in the *New York Daily Herald* on November 14, 1875, the engine was approaching the Providence train station, when it suddenly exploded, hurling all five men aboard quite a distance from the engine. "They were all hurled with terrible force from the engine, and [Fiske was] injured by the fire and escaping steam and also by the fragments of the locomotive." Following the accident, Fiske remained in critical condition and eventually died two weeks later.

21-year-old John Knowles was found over 100 feet from the engine. He was on the train without permission, trying to learn the duties of a train engineer in hopes of obtaining future employment. His medical condition after the blast was extremely serious. The newspaper said, "Everything was done to alleviate his sufferings, but his condition baffled all medical skill, and at six o'clock this morning, death put an end to his sufferings." In addition, the fireman, James Thomas, was "terribly scalded about the breast and lower part of his body." Most of the other persons injured were not as badly hurt.

An inquiry into the accident was conducted, and investigators guessed that the explosion may have been caused "by either a high pressure of steam or from a lack of water in the boiler." The locomotive's boiler had been in use seven or eight years and was the second one installed in the *Matt Morgan*. No defects were believed to exist in the boiler prior to the explosion.

Thus, it happened that the accident in 1875 ended up resulting in the ghostly apparition ten years later. After the appearance of the "ghost" in 1885, the local newspaper introduced some confusion into the narrative by misidentifying the locomotive engineer that had died in the previous accident. An article published after the ghostly sighting gave the dead engineer's name as "Giles," when in fact the name was William Fiske. None of the victims of the 1875 accident were named "Giles," and so it is uncertain where this confusion came from.

Also, the accident that happened in 1875 was not described accurately. The reporters stated that a bridge had been wiped out by flooding and the locomotive had tumbled off the tracks, falling on its side and trapping the engineer under it. Possibly this story was based on another accident that happened nearby, as these sorts of stories were quite common and were often confused. The 1875 accident was, as previously described, a locomotive explosion.

So, what was the ghostly form that appeared to the engineer ten years after the accident? What was this "ghost" attempting to do by preventing the engineer from slowing the train? We may never know.

7

GHOST HILL

1882
NEAR DALLAS, TEXAS

There is a spot about 25 miles south of Dallas, Texas, that in the late 19th Century was known as "Ghost Hill," due to a reported haunting in the area that resulted after a railroad worker was killed in an accident. According to the June 7, 1890 edition of the *Topeka (Kansas) Lance*, Ghost Hill was the location of a siding, which is a short section of track that is set apart from the main line and is used for a variety of purposes. In 1890, the site was marked by a sign with the station's name on it – "Ghost Hill."

Located between the small towns of Palmer and Farris, the supposedly haunted site was situated on "a singular hill in the prairie black lands." The *Lance* said, "It is covered with oak and pecan as tall as Kentucky trees. The locality, though a hill, is always wet. The ground is muddy, and the air murky."

According to the 1890 account, when passing trains approached this spot, they often heard train whistles and bells that seemed to be alerting the crew about a train that was approaching to cross in front of them. Terrified about a possible collision, the train crew would set the brakes and quickly bring their locomotive to a stop – only to discover that no other trains were anywhere nearby and that their own train's engineer had not given any of the signals they claimed to have heard.

According to the *Topeka Lance*, "At night, while passing: this point, time and again has the whistle called for brakes and the bell rung for imaginary crossings. The train men, after setting the brakes, would be terrified to learn that the engineer had not given the signals. More than one crew has incontinently abandoned the service of the company after such experience, not caring to ride over Ghost Hill with the spirit of a fireman killed there many years ago tugging away at bell and whistle." A "fireman" manages the fire in a steam locomotive's boiler to keep the engine running safely.

According to another newspaper account published in in 1890, the death of the fireman happened in about 1882: "Ghost Hill on the line of the Central Railroad between Palmer and Ferris took its name from a superstition among railroad men. About eight years ago an accident occurred on the hill in which a brakeman lost his life and ever since that time it has been claimed by train men that the brakeman's ghost haunted the spot, and as trains would run by, would ring the engine bell.

This tale became current, and the place has ever since been known as Ghost Hill."

During this time period, Ghost Hill was well known to the railroad workers of the region, and many of them were not happy about having to pass through this point, especially at night. This fear sometimes had interesting side effects, such as was reported in the April 6, 1890 edition of the *Fort Worth Daily Gazette.*

According to the newspaper, the fireman of a train that was scheduled to pass through Ghost Hill decided to have a bit of fun at the expense of a passenger named George Ely. As the train approached Ghost Hill, Ely had dozed off, and the fireman sprang into action. What happened next is described in the newspaper account:

"The grade at Ghost Hill is a heavy one, and a freight train makes the ascent almost at a snail's pace. This fact enabled the fireman to get in his work. He blackened his face with coal dust, tied a big white rag about his head and made himself look as horrible as possible. Dropping from the engine to the ground, he ran ahead of the train and with his lantern flagged the engineer to stop. The whistle shrieked out 'down brakes,' and this aroused Ely, who as the train pulled up to the fireman, saw what he at once concluded to be the dead brakeman's ghost. With an exclamation of horror, he scrambled over the tender and back over the long line of freight cars to the caboose which by this time was just where the engine was when he started back. As he started down the side of the car to get inside, the same sight of the brakeman's ghost swinging his lantern met his eyes again. This was too much for him, and he dropped in a dead faint to the ground."

George Ely awoke a while later, safe and sound inside the caboose and discovered that the train had already passed the Ghost Hill site. He soon realized that he had been the target of a practical joke, but he "owned up like a man." The newspaper article added that he swore he would never again travel over Ghost Hill in the night!

8

GHOST ON THE TRACKS

DECEMBER 1871
PORTSMOUTH, VIRGINIA

During America's Old West, there seemed to be quite a number of railroad workers claiming to have seen ghosts. But, among the many odd stories, the following tale is especially bizarre.

In the December 7, 1871 edition of the *Brownstown (Indiana) Banner* there appeared the strange story of a ghostly apparition in Portsmouth, Virginia, that manifested upon the railroad tracks, causing locomotives to engage brakes, only to find no trace of anybody being anywhere near where the specter was seen.

The newspaper tells the story of one particular instance when the crew of a freight train spotted a man lying on the tracks. The man's body was lying within fifteen feet of a gas light, and therefore was clearly visible to the members of the train's crew.

The railroad workers were certain that it was a drunken man who had fallen asleep on the tracks. The locomotive slowed and finally stopped about three feet away from the prone body. All of the train's crew later testified that they could clearly make out the prostrate form of the man lying on the tracks just ahead of them.

Several crewmembers dismounted the train and headed toward the man in order to remove him from the tracks. However, as they approached the body, it suddenly vanished.

A Railroad Ghost.

A Virginia paper has the following: "Portsmouth, Va., has a ghost. A few nights ago, about one o'clock, as the freight train on the Seaboard road, on London street, was approaching Court street, the engineer and others on the engine saw a man lying on the track at the Court street crossing, east side. Thinking it was a drunken man, the train was stopped, and several persons got down off the engine to remove him, but to their surprise found no one there. The apparition vanished as they approached it. The engine was within three feet of him when the train came to a halt, and everybody on the engine saw him, and are willing to make oath to the fact. He was lying within fifteen feet of a gas-light. Whether it was the spirit of some one departed, we are unable to say, but three or four reliable gentlemen are willing to make oath to the correctness of the fact that he was lying on the track, and vanished as they went to remove him."

Brownstown (Indiana) Banner of December 7, 1871, p.6.

Terror on the Train!

The *Brownstown Banner* said, "Whether it was the spirit of someone departed, we are unable to say, but three or four reliable gentlemen are willing to make oath to the correctness of the fact that he was lying on the track, and vanished as they went to remove him."

The location of this incident was given "as the freight train on the Seaboard Road, on London Street, was approaching Court Street" in Portsmouth, Virginia. Due to the frequent arrival of incoming and outgoing freight for the ships at harbor, the area was crisscrossed by railroad tracks, and freight trains operated on a regular basis.

Portsmouth Harbor in 1843.

The case of the "railroad ghost" was commented on in several newspapers of the time, but apparently there were no further occurrences of the same phenomenon after the one that was mentioned in the December 1871 article.

9

THE GHASTLY GHOUL

MARCH 1874
BURLINGTON, IOWA

The psychic phenomenon experienced in Burlington, Iowa, in March 1874 would probably be classified as a "poltergeist" today. A poltergeist is defined as "a ghost or other supernatural being supposedly responsible for physical disturbances such as loud noises and objects thrown around."

These strange occurrences were first reported at the paint shops of the Burlington and Missouri River Railway in Burlington. It was the middle of March in 1874 when the railway company's night watchman began experiencing a series of unexplained phenomena beginning at the midnight hour each evening. The March 19, 1874 edition of the *Burlington (Iowa) Weekly Hawk-Eye* said, "A RAILROAD GHOST. It is invisible but noisy. Its bones are marrowless. Its flesh is cold. And there is no speculation in its eyes that it glares at the watchman with. The ghastly ghoul of the graveyard has broken out in Burlington and devotes his leisure hours to making things lively at the paint shops of the Burlington and Missouri River Railway."

The newspaper pointed out that although this "ghastly ghoul" was invisible, it nonetheless seemed to manifest itself all around the area in the form of pounding noises, slamming doors, falling objects, and so on. "Suddenly with a harsh clangor the doors of the shop clang open, hurled by invisible, unearthly hands...."

(Courtesy OurIowaHeritage.com)

"Then the ghost rattles a car door, and the faithful guardian of the shops hastens to the spot, but finds no one there, and while he looks, lo! the ghastly spook pounds on a car wheel with a coupling link. So, he strays up and down the shops and the yard, the watchman following every sound, seeking the intruder, and finding nothing."

The description continued, "It kicks at the windows and slams the doors and dances unearthly double-shuttles on the tops of the cars. It makes the life of the lone man who night after night is hunting the spirit a burden to him."

The newspaper article further explained that the area where all these spectral manifestations were occurring was very forlorn and frightening. "Down the long dark vista of the track, the signal lamps burn dimly, with a strange unearthly light. The embers raked from the furnace of some locomotive gleam fitfully with the breath of the night wind, and cast grotesque inhuman shadows on the gloomy buildings and the cars on the side-track. From every corner, every angle, every hidden nook, shrouded in deepest impenetrable gloom, dark shadowy shapes at every motion of the lantern, that mock its feeble rays. The shops rise black and lonely out of the darkness at their feet, and over all a death-like silence hangs heavy and solemn, and oppressive as a pall. The echo of a footstep would be company, but the strained attention hears no sound, save the sighing of the night wind. So lonesome, so desolate, so deserted is the place that the world seems thousands of miles away."

Burlington & Missouri River Railroad Stock Certificate, circa 1870.

Another interesting detail mentioned in the newspaper article was that before the phenomenon began every evening, the watchman's lantern suddenly flared up with a blue light. "The lonely watchman, pacing his weary rounds, feels homesick as he notices the light in his lantern burn blue. He waits with bated breath for the manifestations which well he knows that ominous symptom prefaces."

Although the article was written in somewhat of a tongue-in-cheek manner, it seemed obvious that the reporter was following up on actual spooky happenings that had been reported in town. Clearly, something out of the ordinary was going on that had the earmarks of poltergeist activity – or so it would seem based on what is known of the incident.

A Haunted Locomotive.

Northern Pacific locomotive No. 350, which now hauls the regular daily passenger train between Butte and Helena, bears the proud distinction of being haunted. About a year ago it was pulling a tea express over the Northern Pacific and jumped the track and fell over a steep embankment, killing its engineer and fireman. Since that time it has been haunted by the wraiths of the unfortunate men, and no earthly power seems able to drive them away.

Night before last it was being cleaned in the Butte roundhouse, and the two engine-wipers who were at work upon it heard the door of its firebox open and shut violently several times, although there was no living person in the cab at the time. One of the wipers securely fastened the door with his own hands, and then, with his companion, awaited developments. They saw the door shake violently for a moment and then swing wide open, and after remaining thus for a moment close again with a loud bang. Nobody was in the cab, and there was a fire in the box.

No. 350 is known on the Northern Pacific as "the haunted engine."

Butte (Montana) Semi Weekly Miner of July 28, 1886, p.1.

10

LOCOMOTIVE NO. 13

In November 1885, near Missoula, Montana, two trains of the Northern Pacific Railroad collided, resulting in five deaths, two injuries, and the destruction of two engines, a dozen cars, and "a considerable quantity of merchandise." One of the engines ("No. 13") involved in the crash was later rebuilt and returned to service, and it became known as "the haunted locomotive." People said it was haunted by the spirits of the men who died in the horrific 1885 collision.

The tragic story of the haunted locomotive began at 6 a.m. on Friday, November 27, 1885 at a location 13 miles east of Missoula, Montana. An eastbound "tea" train and the westbound No. 13 express freight train came together on a sharp curve. The newspaper said, "Both trains were running at a high rate of speed and the windings of the road prevented any knowledge of their approach toward each other until a second or two before the engines struck."

Michael Rech, 35, the engineer of the No. 13, did not have time to get off his seat in the cab before the two engines came together. "He was caught in the wreck and held down by the heavy machinery, while the steam from the boiler and the fire from the furnace were scalding and burning him, leaving but little skin on his body. He survived all this, however, and retained consciousness until eleven o'clock, that morning, dying at the hospital here just after his arrival."

In an inquest following the crash, engineer Rech, a native of Belgium, was found partly responsible for the accident for failing to heed a signal given to him as he passed a train station in Wallace, Montana, shortly before the collision.

Also killed on Locomotive 13 was the fireman, Alvin S. Moffat, a 28-year-old native of Pennsylvania. "His arm was torn from his body at the elbow, his legs and back were broken, and was badly scalded. He was a new man on the road. It is said he had a premonition of death and did not want to go on this trip, but the regular fireman was sick. Moffatt had to take the place."

A third man died horribly in the No. 13. He was 22-year-old William A. Andrews, who was riding the rear of the tender of No. 13 when the crash came. He was crushed "almost to a jelly," with the top of his head being taken entirely off.

The other two fatalities were on the other train. "Norman Rice, fireman of the tea train, being on the side against the embankment, could not get to the other side of the engine quick enough to jump off and was caught in the wreck. His left leg was badly crushed above the knee and he received serious internal injuries, On Saturday his leg was amputated and Sunday morning he died in the hospital here, his body being embalmed and forwarded to friends in San Francisco the next day."

Also killed in the tea train was Thomas Devine, head brakeman. "It is supposed he was on the first or second car and when the collision occurred, he was thrown forward and fell under the wreck of the engines. He was crushed and burned almost beyond recognition, and both legs were severed from the body."

A notable survivor of the tea train was the engineer, J. B. Waite, who saw the collision about to happen and jumped out of the moving train. The newspaper said Waite "caught a reflection of the headlight of the freight and jumped from his engine, falling upon the rocks which form the road bed and receiving only some scratches and bruises, the lightness of his injuries being quite remarkable."

Following this horrible tragedy, Locomotive No. 13 was rebuilt and returned to service within a year. Its number was changed to No. 350, and it took on the duty of hauling the regular daily passenger train between Butte, Montana, and Helena, Montana. However, despite the number change and the amount of time that had passed since the crash, this locomotive was known as "the haunted locomotive."

The July 28, 1886 edition of the *Butte (Montana) Semi-Weekly Miner*, said this about the engine, "About a year ago it was pulling an express over the Northern Pacific and jumped the track and fell over a steep embankment, killing the engineer and fireman. Since that time, it has been haunted by the wraiths of the unfortunate men, and no earthly power seems able to drive them away."

The *Semi-Weekly Miner* noted that a number of unexplained incidents had happened involving No. 350, including one that happened on the evening of July 26, 1886 at the Butte train roundhouse where the No. 350 was being cleaned by railroad workers. "Night before last it was being cleaned in the Butte roundhouse, and the two engine wipers [cleaners] who were at work upon it heard the door of the firebox open and shut violently several times, although there was no living person in the cab at the time. One of the wipers securely fastened the door with his own hands, and then, with his companion, awaited developments. They saw the door shake violently for a moment and then swing wide open, and after remaining thus for a moment closed again with a loud bang. Nobody was in the cab, and there was a fire in the box. No.350 is known on the Northern Pacific as 'the haunted engine.'"

This was only one of a number of unusual happenings that continued to plague Engine No. 350. Was it the spirits of the men who were so horribly mangled and killed on November 27, 1885? The mystery of Montana's haunted locomotive remains to this day.

Statue of John Chisum and Old Ruidoso in Roswell, NM. (John LeMay)

11

CURSED STEER CAUSES TRAIN CRASH

1888
AMARILLO, TEXAS

Our next tale involves a cursed steer causing a terrible train wreck in Texas. But, before getting to the wreck itself, let's review some history. The cursed steer was none other than Old Ruidoso, the most mythic of John Chisum's Longhorn steers. John Chisum was himself a legendary cattle baron in New Mexico who owned more land and cattle than just about anyone in North America in the late 1870s. Under Chisum's employ at one time was even Billy the Kid himself. As for Old Ruidoso, he was what was known as a "decoy" steer in that due to his immense size he was used by cattle drivers to lead the herd on long drives. To show the steer's "leadership status" a long rail was burned into their hide to differentiate them from the other large steers.

Being a decoy steer had an additional meaning, being that Ruidoso was also a decoy for rustlers because he had a hidden rail brand on the steer's inside flank. In essence, this made it easier for Chisum to catch a rustler from a legal standpoint as the rustler probably didn't see the brand in the first place, a rather dishonest trick if there ever was one. One of the first to come across Old Ruidoso was outlaw Jesse Evans, who was far too wise in the ways of rustling to abscond with Ruidoso. Instead, he branded him with a question mark. Other would-be rustlers caught on, and added their own brands to show just what they thought of the dirty trick. Reportedly, within a few weeks Old Ruidoso was covered in brands, some of which were in the shapes of snakes and scorpions.

Depiction of Ruidoso from *The Cattleman Magazine.*

Old Ruidoso's most notorious brand came from "Pecos" Bob Olinger, who was riding along the Pecos River when he spied Old Ruidoso near its banks. Olinger roped Old Ruidoso and then branded him with a skull and crossbones and placed a curse on him. As he did this, the then unnamed steer let out a bellow unlike any other, and so Olinger dubbed him Ruidoso which meant noisy, and said, "Your appearance in the roundups from Horsehead Crossing to the Bosque Grande on the Pecos shall be a curse, and I wish you could live a hundred years. But when you are dead and gone, I hope that terrible bellow of yours will haunt the people. I know that this curse I am bestowing on you will contribute to the population of every boot-hill cemetery along the Pecos." Some tellers of this tall tale even like to said Olinger's "curse" was what helped to start the whole Lincoln County War, for it was shortly after Olinger branded Old Ruidoso that the war broke out on the range.

But was Bob Olinger really the one who branded Old Ruidoso, or was Olinger merely the chosen villain by campfire storytellers? Olinger, it should be noted, aside from being Billy the Kid's tormenter in jail, was also on the side of the "bad guys" during the Lincoln County War. So vile was Olinger, reportedly his own mother was glad when he finally bit the dust. Olinger being on the opposite side of John Chisum and his men could have branded Old Ruidoso out of spite, but there's still no real way of proving it.

Illustration of Billy the Kid gunning down Bob Olinger.

Either way, the curse of Old Ruidoso would come back to haunt Olinger in the form of outlaw Billy the Kid. When Billy was being held at the Lincoln County Courthouse sentenced to hang for cattle rustling, Olinger was the Kid's constant tormenter. It should also be noted that Olinger had earlier killed the Kid's good friend John Jones in a shootout. The Kid got his revenge after he shot and killed guard J.W. Bell while Olinger was out. Billy picked up Olinger's own buckshot loaded shotgun and waited for Olinger from the second story window. "Hello, Bob," the Kid said casually when Olinger came into range. Olinger looked up and got a face full of buckshot killing him after which Billy rode out of town.

In 1886, Old Ruidoso wandered into a cattle roundup on the West Mora Arroyo north of Roswell. When the cursed steer was spotted, one cowpoke said to another, "I expect hell will pop. I see the hoodoo steer over there." And within twenty minutes two of the cowboys had gotten into an argument and one shot the other. Another tale, set just outside of Roswell at a place called Pilky Flats, says Ruidoso was spotted grazing with old man Pilky's milk cows. The next day the whole Pilky clan was found dead with doctors claiming it was due to poisoned alkali milk.

Modern illustration of old Ruidoso by Roswell artist Chris Casey.

Among other alleged deaths at the hooves of Old Ruidoso was one Zack Light, who informed the residents of Seven Rivers that he had just seen the cursed steer on the trail. That night Light's time came, and he was killed in a poker game. These were only the beginning of Old Ruidoso's reign of terror however. Soon his bad luck would result in the relocation of an entire Texas town.

In 1888 Old Ruidoso was deemed public property as John Chisum had passed away long ago and a law had been passed that all defaced branded cattle stock be deemed public property. As such, several cattlemen got together and decided that Ruidoso should be dealt with once and for all and he would be taken to Amarillo for the slaughter. As no trail bosses wanted to take part in a cattle drive that Ruidoso was a part of, a popular trail boss named Colonel Jack Potter agreed to drive Ruidoso to his final resting place.

In Potter's mind the drive to Amarillo had been one of the straightest in history, but the drovers had other stories. To them the drive was filled with bad luck, and at night they would gather around the campfire to talk about the day's events and ponder shooting Old Ruidoso right between the eyes. It seems the old steer mostly made them nervous, nothing of any consequence seemed to happen during the drive, and they all reached Amarillo, a relatively new town along the Texas Panhandle, without incident.

They all happily waved adios to Old Ruidoso and his herd, ecstatic to be free from any future bad luck. This truly was to be Old Ruidoso's last drive. Upon arriving by train in Kansas City, Old Ruidoso and the rest of the cattle would be slaughtered. But Old Ruidoso had other plans. When Potter and his men returned to Fort Sumner after seeing Ruidoso off on the train from Amarillo, they got the news. Just ten hours out of Amarillo, the train carrying Old Ruidoso had derailed and wrecked. No one knew why, but several men and cattle were killed. Most of the cattle escaped, and included in those missing was Old Ruidoso. The town of Amarillo was so spooked by the incident that they too worried that they had fallen under Ruidoso's curse. So superstitious were they that they even moved the whole town out of the lake bed where it originally stood to its present location today.

Naturally, there is some truth to the train wreck story. For instance, in terms of the history of Amarillo, it did indeed start as a little cow-town along the railroad in 1887. Originally, it was called Oneida before switching to Amarillo and the town did move from its original spot in the year 1888. However, it was not due to a train crash. Two local businessmen, Henry B. Sanborn and Joseph F. Glidden, decided to begin buying land east of the current townsite due to the fact that their current property resided on low ground prone to flooding in the rainy season. As stated before, this decision was made in 1888, the same year that Old Ruidoso took the train.

You would also think that a story as sensational as a train wreck caused by a cursed cow would be easy to find. While there two Texas train wreck stories in newspapers appearing in late 1888, Colonel Potter never specified where his herd was being shipped, only that a cattle broker out of Kansas City, Missouri was handling the transaction. As such, it's difficult to discern which of the two wrecks might have been the one involving Old Ruidoso.

The Colorado Special along the Fort Worth Denver Railway c.1929.

Per the *Weekly Times-Democrat* of October 13, 1888, a terrible train wreck occurred along the Fort Worth and Denver Railroad seven miles north of the town of Vernon, Texas. Two separate cattle trains were on the tracks early that morning when the "air was full of mist and fog." Both trains were "coming south a short distance apart" when a "hot box caused the first freight to stop."

The article reported that the conductor, identified as a man named Pitzer, "sent a man back to flag the second train." However, due to the mist and fog, the "engineer of the second train could not see the train ahead until within four car lengths. He reverted his engine and called to his fireman and others on the engine to jump." As this happened, the caboose of the first freight, housing six men who were sleeping, "was split in two, the sides thrown on the embankment and the top carried some distance and pitched on the bank. The engine of the second train was thrown across the tracks as was the tender." The paper went on to report that one hundred head of cattle were killed along with a worker named George Lake who was killed instantly. Many more men were injured.

Terror on the Train!

Along the lines of this wreck happening under the curse of Old Ruidoso, the paper specifically noted that the accident occurred at 3:30 AM. Though most people are taught that midnight is the "witching hour," investigators of the supernatural have noted that most paranormal encounters, be they involving Bigfoot, ghosts, or even alien abductions, typically occur at or around 3:30 in the morning. Coincidentally, the unusual name of Pitzer, the conductor, was also the name of John Chisum's brother, Pitzer Chisum. Coincidence? Probably.

> **Fatal Accident on the Fort Worth and Denver Road—One Person Killed and Several Wounded.**
>
> Special to The Times-Democrat.
>
> VERNON, Tex., Oct. 10.—A wreck occurred on the Fort Worth and Denver Railroad, seven miles north of Vernon, at 3:30 o'clock this morning. Two special trains loaded with cattle shipped from Rivers for Henrietta were coming south a short distance apart. A hot box caused the first freight to stop. Conductor Pitzer sent a man back to flag the second train. The air was full of mist and fog.
>
> The engineer of the second train could not see the train ahead until within four car lengths. He reversed his engine and called to his fireman and others on the engine to jump. The caboose of the first freight, in which were six men asleep, was split in two, the sides thrown on the embankment and the top carried some distance and pitched on the bank.

The fact that the account stated that the accident occurred ten hours after the train departed Amarillo also lines up with Potter's story that the wreck happened ten hours out of Amarillo. Today, Vernon is about three to three and a half hours away by car on modern highways from Amarillo. Considering trains back then traveled at around 50 mph, and accounting for stops for water etc., it probably took around ten hours for a train to reach Vernon from Amarillo.

In any case, Old Ruidoso got the last laugh. No one knows how or when Ruidoso died after his great escape, but his ghost soon began haunting the ranges of New Mexico and Texas. West of the Pecos, settlers began telling tales of the bloodcurdling bellows of a steer they could hear up in the mountains. They began to say it was Old Ruidoso returned to his old stomping grounds...

12

BALTIMORE'S HAUNTED LOCOMOTIVE

1885
BALTIMORE, MARYLAND

Another haunted locomotive story comes to us from 1885 in Baltimore, Maryland, and was reported in the *Baltimore Times*, as well as other newspapers of the era. The story came from a veteran engineer with the Baltimore and Ohio Railroad, who told the *Times* that he was previously the engineer on the "haunted locomotive," which was part of the Pennsylvania Railroad Company when the incidents occurred.

The engineer, whom we will call Jones, said, "I ran one on the Pennsylvania railroad for about a year that was haunted. My engine was a good one, but had some very curious actions at times. I believe a locomotive can be haunted."

Jones went on to explain that the previous engineer had been killed in a train collision near Cresson, Pennsylvania. The dead engineer lived in a small house located just west of Altoona, Pennsylvania. Every time the dead engineer had passed his house, he "slowed his engine … and waived his hand at his wife and children, who stood in the door and bowed and smiled at him."

After his demise, the locomotive would behave strangely every time it approached the former home of the dead engineer. It seemed that an unknown force would take control of the train, and the train would slow down as it used to do when the dead man was in control of it.

Jones said, "The man who ran the engine before I took her was killed in a little collision beyond Cresson. He lived in a little house just west of Altoona. In my run coming east I always passed this house about 9 o'clock at night. Just before reaching it for several nights I noticed that my engine commenced to slow up more than intended. I began to think. I was growing nervous, and my hand was no longer true in guiding the throttle."

Jones' story continued, "But it never occurred anywhere else. The effect made on my mind by the circumstance became very unpleasant. After a while I realized that there was some power helping me at the throttle. When I reached that place, I mentioned it to my fireman, and made him try it. He was convinced that my impression was right."

Terror on the Train!

On another occasion, while passing the former engineer's house, the train's whistle suddenly gave several loud blasts. The engineer thought that his fireman had pulled the cord, but the fireman denied it. The same thing happened two or three more times, and each time, the crew could not see any hand pulling the cord to make the whistle sound. Yet it sounded.

Jones said, "Well, you may be sure I didn't like this sort of thing. At last, a creepy feeling began to crawl all over me when approaching the dead engineer's house. One dark night in June 1881, I made up my mind to balk [thwart] the ghost."

Jones explained, "I called the fireman in the cab and both of us grasped the throttle, slowed up to the proper speed, and held on to it firmly. We felt something tugging at it, but we were too strong for it. Suddenly the throttle was wrenched from our hands and pulled out to the utmost limit. Away bounded the train down the grade into Altoona, the whistle shrieking like a demon. Before could get away from the ghost the train had attained great speed, and we ran half way through the city before we could slow up."

Jones continued, "A switchman for B&O [Baltimore & Ohio Railroad] saw us coming and switched us on a side track beyond the Logan House, where we wrecked two or three cattle cars and damaged the engine. The incident caused great commotion among the people living along the tracks, and the company censured me for it."

After his several run-ins with the mysterious forces on this particular locomotive, Jones decided to quit his job and return to work for the Baltimore and Ohio Railroad, where he had previously worked. He told the newspaper, "As I couldn't be responsible for a ghost's antics, I threw up the job and came back to the B&O."

When asked if he thought the locomotive was haunted by the spirit of the dead engineer, Jones replied, "I think so. He always slowed his engine while nearing his house, and waved his hand at his wife and children, who stood in the door and bowed and smiled at him. He might have raised all that rumpus. He must have gotten mad because I didn't let him have his way."

This story was reported in the July 12, 1885 edition of the *Wheeling (W. Va.) Sunday Register*. It cited the original source as the *Baltimore Times* newspaper.

13

GHOSTLY WOMEN ON THE TRACKS

1881- 1883
COLORADO AND PENNSYLVANIA

There are many stories of ghosts warning train crews of an impending disaster. This chapter examines three very similar incidents. The first, from Denver, Colorado, is one of the most intriguing, as it involves a case where apparently a ghostly apparition managed to actually save a train from becoming involved in a head-on collision with another train! In this case, the ghostly apparition took the form of a woman holding a signal lantern, as if trying to warn the train.

The story came from the *Denver Times* newspaper of April 1881, and it was told to the newspaper by an old-time railroad worker that we will refer to as Mr. Smith.

Smith said, "I knew an engineer once who could not help going to sleep on his engine, try as he would. Nothing would cure him. He was on the edge of an accident all the time, and the thing got talked about so that the general officers heard about it and were going to let him out. He begged so hard, though, that they concluded to let him run a little longer, and see if he couldn't cure himself."

Shortly after the engineer was given another chance to keep his job, he had a very frightening encounter. Smith said, "One night, when his train was booming along, a signal was out ordering him to stop for telegraphic instructions, but he happened to be asleep when they passed by the station and shot right by. A few minutes later he awoke, shook himself and began attending to business. It was very dark, and, luckily for him slowed up a little. Just as he did so he looked ahead and saw what seemed to be a signal lantern ahead on the track. He stopped at once, but as he did so the lantern disappeared."

Wondering about the source of the mysterious lantern, the engineer started up the locomotive again and began moving. Almost immediately, he saw the lantern again, only this time he saw the form of what appeared to be a woman standing behind the lantern. "By this time, he was thoroughly bewildered and a little frightened, and sent his fireman ahead on the truck where the lantern had seemed to be. There was nothing there."

Smith said, "The train was started once more, and again the lantern light flashed on. He watched it more closely this time, and it seemed to him that the lantern moved with the train, keeping the same speed and the same distance. The cold sweat came on his forehead, and he grew thoroughly frightened."

Terror on the Train!

For a third time, the lantern light appeared, and this time it seemed to be following the train, keeping a certain distance behind it. Fearful and confused, the engineer remembered that he had been asleep when the train passed the last station. He decided to backtrack and head back to the missed station, which he did. Even as the train returned to the station, the mysterious light followed close behind.

Upon reaching the station, the engineer received the telegraph message that he had previously missed, instructing him to switch his train off the main track and leave the road clear for a "white flag" train [a special train not on printed schedules] coming from the opposite direction on the same track. Heeding the instructions, he was barely able to complete the requested task before the other train came thundering around the curve at over 40 miles per hour.

It became clear to the engineer and his crew that the mysterious lantern and the ghostly woman seen with it had saved them from a head-on collision with another train!

A few years after this story, there was another sighting in Colorado of a strange woman appearing in front of a moving train locomotive, this time near Boulder, Colorado.

Train engineer Gene Smith was rounding a deep cut near a train station when he saw "the figure of woman dressed in white flying across the track." The ghostly figure then laid down upon the tracks as if to await the train's impact. Smith said he tried to apply the brakes, but it was too late. "I gave the whistle. It was an echo of the despairing wail that rose from my heart. I closed my eyes, but we struck nothing."

As in the Denver incident, the ghostly figure vanished.

"Looking out from my engine a moment later, I saw before me, floating up and with the hand waving mockingly at me, the figure which I had just seen lying prostrate on the tracks."

The newspaper added, "J. D. Crowley, who runs another train over the same route, confirms Smith's story. Both are men of unquestioned veracity. There is much apprehension among trainmen over that branch, and it is said there is a strong demand for rabbits' feet and other talismans."

Two years later, in 1883, the ghostly woman of the railroad tracks appeared again, this time in Royer's Ford, Pennsylvania, in the area known as the Schuylkill Valley. The incident was reported by David Lowe, train engineer with the Reading Railroad, which was based in Philadelphia.

Lowe reported leaving from Pottstown, Pennsylvania, during a very bad snow storm. A newspaper account in the *Clyde (Ohio) Enterprise* said, "His sturdy engine was making thirty miles an hour, as the train swept away from Pottstown through the blinding snowstorm. The wind chased the flying express like mad, catching up clouds of snowflakes and sweeping them in a hundred fantastic shapes through the midnight air like shrouded spirits, to which the shrill scream of the tempest seemed to supply a supernatural voice."

"The night," said the engineer, "was as dark as a mountain of coal, and I and my fireman, William Miller, had to keep a sharp lookout ahead. I had heard of ghosts on railroad tracks, but I had never seen any. In fact, I don't believe in ghosts or spirits or anything of that kind; and I don't say that what we saw was a ghost... but it was very queer, and I tell you it made me feel mighty funny. The snow was swirling up in front of us, and it was impossible to see the track very far ahead."

As Lowe kept the locomotive moving forward, he and Miller suddenly spotted a "red light" up ahead in the distance. The light was not directly on the railroad tracks but slightly off to one side. Fearing that it was a signal light warning of a problem in the tracks ahead, Lowe slowed the locomotive way down and moved ahead very cautiously.

"When we had gotten within a few yards of the light, it was swung across the rails, and something like a woman dressed in white stepped on the track."

Boggled by the ghostly apparition, Lowe and Miller thought that perhaps there had been some sort of accident, and the woman needed help. Lowe brought the train to a stop, but as the two men were dismounting from the locomotive, the figure of the woman and the red light both suddenly disappeared.

"It just seemed to vanish. Were we frightened? Well, you see, the storm, and the ghost-like things made by the drifting snow, the dark night, and this mysterious apparition were calculated to make us feel very uneasy. It was about the strangest thing I ever saw in my life, and a man in a locomotive cab sees some very queer sights."

In told the story of this strange incident, the *Clyde Enterprise* pointed out that it occurred in an area of Pennsylvania that had long been known for strange phenomena: "The enginemen of the Reading Railroad report strange things from the Schuylkill Valley, about Fort Kennedy Station and Royer's Ford. Witches, ghosts, and goblins are said to haunt the country at night, stopping trains by waving spirit red lights across the track, frightening the train hands with their ghoulish cries, and even at times squatting like imps of darkness on the rear platform. When the nights are dark and stormy, the frightened shriek of the engine, as it darts through the darkness like a great fire-eyed cyclops, often arouses a spirit from the very center of the track."

Terror on the Train!

Ghostly Track-Walkers.

The enginemen of the Reading Railroad report strange things from the Schuylkill Valley, about Fort Kennedy Station and Royer's Ford. Witches, ghosts, and goblins are said to haunt the country at night, stopping trains by waving spirit red lights across the track, frightening the train hands with their ghoulish cries, and even at times squatting like imps of darkness on the rear platform. When the nights are dark and stormy the frightened shriek of the engine, as it darts through the darkness like a great fire-eyed cyclops, often arouses a spirit from the very center of the track. Engineer David Lowe, who left Philadelphia with his train yesterday afternoon, tells a most wonderful story of what he recently saw at Royer's Ford. His sturdy engine was making thirty miles an hour, as the train swept away from Pottstown through the blinding snowstorm. The wind chased the flying express like mad, catching up clouds of snowflakes and sweeping them in a hundred fantastic shapes through the midnight air like shrouded spirits, to which the shrill scream of the tempest seemed to supply a supernatural voice.

In another case reported in Iowa in 1877, a woman who was savagely raped and murdered near some railroad tracks was said to have returned in ghostly form, appearing to passing trains. The apparition was reported by employees of the Chicago, Rock Island, and Pacific Road. According to the *Daily Nonpareil* of Council Bluffs, Iowa (August 22, 1897), these employees claimed their railroad was "haunted by a 'woman in white,' who about the hour of midnight appears and presents a more ghostly spectacle than Wilkie Collins' most thrilling conception." [Wilkie Collins was a British novelist well known for his 1859 mystery novel *The Woman in White*].

The newspaper reported that the strange apparition was seen on the evening of Wednesday, August 15, 1897, by an engineer named Moore on Train No. 9, traveling between Perlee, Iowa, and Pleasant Plain, Iowa.

Engineer Moore saw the woman in white walking up the track toward the engine. He immediately signaled for the brakes and brought his train to a standstill within eight feet of the strange specter. Moore could see its face plainly and was convinced it was a flesh and blood woman. He thought she might be a sleep walker or a mentally disturbed woman.

As soon as the train came to a full stop, the apparition vanished before the engineer's eyes.

On the following two nights, the figure was seen by two other train engineers in the same area. The *Daily Nonpareil* reported, "On Thursday and Friday nights, it was seen at different places between the two towns by engineers Shaffer and Crow, who agree with Moore as to its description, manner of appearance, etc. Since its first visit, the train men have been on the watch, determined to see what it is and how it gets there. They are too brave to be frightened by the apparition, even if it is an inhabitant of the spirit world, but still their curiosity gets away with them, and in their determination to ferret out the mystery, they do stand a little in awe of the fragile form that gives them these mysterious visits."

"The matter is a common topic of conversation among railroad men on the division. Three years ago, a married woman was outraged [raped] in a terrible manner near the place where the white specter has been seen, receiving injuries which caused her death some three weeks after. Now there is a suspicion that one or two parties who know more about the affair than they have ever told, take occasional business trips on the line, and that it is to trouble their conscience that the form appears."

A Haunted Railroad.

The employes of the Chicago, Rock Island and Pacific road, on the southwestern division, are having a little sensation of their own which is creating no little excitement along the line. It is claimed that the road is haunted by a "woman in white" who about the hour of midnight appears and presents a more ghostly spectacle than Wilkie Collins' most thrilling conception. According to the Fairfield *Ledger*, the shape, whatever it may be, was seen on Wednesday night of last week, by engineer Moore, on train No. 9, between Perlee and Pleasant Plain. It was walking up the track toward the engine, and the careful engineer, thinking it a thing of flesh and blood, actually whistled for brakes and almost brought his train to a stand still. Just as the form was within a few feet of him it disappeared. He saw a face plainly, and supposed it either that of a lunatic or a somnambulist. On Thursday and Friday nights it was seen at different places between the two towns by engineers Shaffer and Crow, who agree with Moore as to its description, manner of appearance, etc. Since its first visit the train men have been on the watch, determined to see what it is and how it gets there. They are too brave to be frightened by the apparition, even if it is an inhabitant of the spirit world, but still their curiosity gets away with them, and in their determination to ferret out the mystery they do stand a little in awe of the fragile form that gives them these mysterious visits.

The matter is a common topic of conversation among railroad men on the division. Three years ago a married woman was outraged in a terrible manner near the place where the white specter has been seen, receiving injuries which caused her death some three weeks after. Now there is a suspicion that one or two parties who know more about the affair than they have ever told, take occasional business trips on the line, and that it is to trouble their conscience that the form appears.

Daily Nonpareil (Council Bluffs, Iowa), 8-22-1897, p. 4.

14

UFO ON THE
RAILROAD TRACKS

1883
CANAJOHARIE, NEW YORK

The authors have previously written about hundreds of unidentified flying object sightings in the 19th century, including many that were described by witnesses as bright floating orbs of light. These orbs did not float about randomly, but rather seemed to be under intelligent control. They often followed a straight course, as if they had purpose in their direction.

A similar incident was reported in the tiny village of Canajoharie in New York state in the summer of 1883. The strange story appeared in a number of U.S. newspapers, including the *Daily Register* of Wheeling, West Virginia, on August 17, 1883. The article opened with the declaration: "Excitement runs high at Canajoharie, owing to the nightly appearance of a ghostly, mysterious light along the [New York] Central railroad track."

Villagers reported seeing the strange light usually appearing near Fort Canajoharie, a historic British fort built in 1747 during King George's War.

The newspaper article said, "The light starts from the old fort, and is at first very small. It gradually increases in size, and goes down the railroad track about three feet from the ground."

Interestingly, the light seemed small when it first appeared, but as it moved down the railroad tracks, it seemed to grow in size. From three feet off the ground, the light would sometimes dip down to just inches above the ground as it moved along the tracks. Other times it would rise as high as thirty feet above the ground.

Another strange detail about the light is that some witnesses claim they saw what appeared to be a human hand near the light, as if holding it. "The night watchmen say that a hand can be distinguished about it. Sometimes the light goes bounding down the track, and again rises thirty feet in the air."

The appearance of this phenomenon did occasionally disrupt the train traffic in the area, as train engineers sometimes saw the moving light and thought it might be a signal light warning them of danger ahead on the tracks. "Several trains, including the Atlantic express, have been stopped by the light, believing it to be a danger signal."

Terror on the Train!

A PHANTOM HAND

Revealed on a Railroad Track by a
Ghastly Light.

A Mysterious Light on the New York Central Railroad—Great Excitement Among Employes.

AMSTERDAM. N. Y., August 16.—Excitement runs high at Canajoharie, owing to the nightly appearance of a ghostly, mysterious light along the Central railroad track. The light starts from the old fort, and is at first very small. It gradually increases in size, and goes down the railroad track about three feet from the ground. The night watchmen say that

A Hand

can be distinguished about it. Sometimes the light goes bounding down the track, and again rises thirty feet in the air. Several trains, including the Atlantic express, have been stopped by the light, believing it to be a danger signal. It appears about 10:30 P. M., just before the arrival of the fast mail.

Fifty persons lay in ambush in the vicinity last night in hopes of ferreting out the matter, but the light did not appear, but the night watchmen and others vouch for the truth of its appearance usually. Railroad men are

Filled With Fear

and superstition, and dread to approach the spot at night. Some say it is a forewarning of a railroad horror to be enacted in the vicinity. Another party of investigators will make another trial to-night.

The Daily Register
(Wheeling, West Virginia)
of August 17, 1883.

The strange light appeared nightly at about 10:30 p.m. and thus seemed to operate on somewhat of a regular schedule. Since the locals knew of its regular appearance, an ad hoc task force was assembled one evening to try to ambush the light and discover its secrets.

The newspaper said, "Fifty persons lay in ambush in the vicinity recently in hopes of ferreting out the matter, but the light did not appear, but the night watchman and others vouch for the truth of its appearance."

The newspaper article concluded by saying, "Usually railroad men are filled with fear and superstition, and dread to approach the spot at night. Some say it is a forewarning of a railroad horror to be enacted in the vicinity."

THE ENTERPRISE.

☞ [Entered in the Post Office at Clyde, Ohio, as second Class Mail Matter.]

CLYDE, MARCH 1, 1883.

Ghostly Track-Walkers.

The Port Kennedy Station ghost, which has for some time been exciting the curiosity of some of the train men and the terror of others, is believed in by more than one of the rugged old engineers. It is said to be

THE SPIRIT OF A TRAMP

who was run over by a train in that locality over ten years ago. Plenty of Reading employes will swear to having seen this phantom. Some of them have shot at it, some even have knocked it on its ghostly head with a cordwood stick, but the bullets went through the scepter without injuring it, and the club only seemed to beat the air. Engineer Charles Welch reports having seen this ghost on Christmas night, and others have encountered it since.

The engineer has since been on the lookout for it again, and on last Saturday night it appeared on the track just below Port Kennedy Station. For a moment he thought it was a real man of flesh and blood. In a second his hand was on the throttle-bar and the brakes were put down, but not in time to prevent the train from running over the mysterious track-walker. The fireman thought that they had killed a wayfarer, although there was no shock. Although the engineer was sure it was the ghost, which could not be harmed even if a dozen trains should run over it, the conductor and some of the hands went back to find the body. There was nothing there, and, although everybody laughed at the engineer when he told them it was the ghost, they all agreed that the affair was awfully strange.

Among the other persons who have come in contact with this reformed spirit of the dead tramp is brakeman George Nelson, who tells a thrilling story of his encounter with it on New Year's eve. He emptied both chambers of his double-barreled gun directly at his face, but it only laughed and floated away on the wings of the howling wind. These and other strange stories are the current gossip of the Thirteenth and Callowhill streets Station, and the night men who pass by the Port Kennedy Station or through Royer's Ford keep a sharp lookout for the ghost of the rail.—*Philadelphia Record.*

15

THE TRAMP ON THE TRACKS

1883

PORT KENNEDY STATION, PENNSYLVANIA

An ever-present danger to train crews in the late 1800s were the hobos and tramps that tended to make their camps and also bed down for the night on railroad tracks. To these transients, the tracks offered a nice, clean, level place to set up camp. Since not a train was in sight when they first arrived, they figured it was safe. Surely, they thought, if a train did come, they would see it and hear it long before it threatened them.

The unfortunate reality was that these tramps would often fall asleep and fail to hear the oncoming train before it trampled them to death, as happened in the 1870s near Port Kennedy Station, Pennsylvania, located 25 miles northwest of Philadelphia. The death of one particular tramp resulted in the legend of the "Port Kennedy Station ghost," which became well known among the railroad workers of the Reading Pennsylvania Train Company.

The March 1, 1883 edition of the *Clyde (Ohio) Enterprise* said, "The Port Kennedy Station ghost, which has for some time been exciting the curiosity of some of the train men and the terror of others, is believed in by more than one of the rugged old engineers. It is said to be the spirit of a tramp who was run over by a train in that locality over ten years ago."

"Plenty of Reading employees will swear to having seen this phantom. Some of them have shot at it, some even hit it on its ghostly head with a cordwood stick, but the bullets went through the specter without injuring it, and the club only seemed to beat the air. Engineer Charles Welch reports having seen this ghost on Christmas night [1882], and others have encountered it since."

The newspaper then related the amazing story of how Engineer Welch encountered the weird apparition again on Saturday, February 24, 1883. "The engineer has since been on the lookout for it again, and on last Saturday night, it appeared on the track just below Port Kennedy Station."

Welch thought that the figure on the tracks ahead of his train was a "real man of flesh and blood" and immediately took steps to bring the locomotive to a stop before striking the apparition. "In a second, his hand was on the throttle bar and the brakes were put down, but not in time to prevent the train from running over the mysterious track-walker."

Terror on the Train!

Although no impact was felt when the train seemed to strike the mysterious figure, the train's fireman was convinced that they had killed somebody on the tracks. The firemen and several other crewmembers dismounted the locomotive and hurried back to the location where the train seemed to have hit the figure.

Not only did they find no body, there was no blood or any evidence whatsoever of a person being struck by the train. Engineer Welch expressed his opinion that it was assuredly the ghost of the dead tramp, which could not be harmed even if a dozen trains should run over it. The train's crew laughed nervously at his suggestion but agreed that the whole affair was awfully strange.

Among the other persons who came in contact with this re-formed spirit of the dead tramp was brakeman George Nelson, who told a thrilling story of his encounter with it on New

Year's Eve [1883]. He emptied both chambers of his double-barreled gun directly at the ghost's face, but it only "laughed" and floated away on the wings of the howling wind.

Port Kennedy Station in 1907.

The newspaper account in the *Clyde Enterprise* summed up the story by saying, "These and other strange stories are the current gossip of the Thirteenth and Callowhill streets Station and the night men who pass by the Port Kennedy Station or through Royer's Ford keep a sharp lookout for the ghost of the rail."

16

MURDER ON THE MARFA EXPRESS

1921
MARFA, TEXAS

Today, Marfa, Texas, is known worldwide for strange lights seen on the outskirts of town. The ghostly orbs of light have been likened to everything from UFOs to witches in flight to perhaps even unknown lifeforms that are bioluminescent. Oddly enough, the infamous lights are indelibly linked to that of the Southern Pacific Railroad, which arrived at Marfa in January 1882. The first serious attempt to discover the origin of the Marfa Lights came about when a railroad engineer named Walter T. Harris used surveyor's methods to find the exact location of the strange lights. However, he was not successful and concluded that the lights might be coming from deep within Mexico.

In 1921 occurred a somewhat famous train accident in Paisano Pass, 12 miles east of Marfa. Due to the fact that it took place near the Marfa Lights, relatively speaking, and involved a mysterious Man in Black, some have lumped the mystery in with UFO phenomena. Whether or not it should be linked to it is debatable, as the connection is tangential.

In any case, the mystery began on the morning of July 8, 1921. A train of the Southern Pacific Railroad, Engine No. 745, was on its way from Sanderson, Texas, to Valentine. At around 5 AM it was going through Paisano Pass when it suddenly came to a stop and the engine room exploded. The explosion propelled the engine car 200 yards from the main track, while the hefty boiler landed about 30 feet away. The force of the explosion even caused the tracks to bend under the stress. The body of the conductor, William Francis Bohlman, was found badly burned, about 60 feet away from the train. Obviously, he didn't survive. Oddly, the other man in the engine car with Bohman was found alive four miles away. No, he didn't get blown there from the explosion, but it was very odd that the man, Charles F. Robinson, a fireman on board the train, was found unconscious and with very few injuries. How did he get there? Being unconscious, he couldn't say.

Photograph of the accident, note the engine car on the left.
[Terrell County Memorial Museum]

While accidents like that did happen with train boilers back then, this one was odd in the fact that this was a brand-new engine, recently finished at the Algiers Shops owned by the Southern Pacific Railroad. Another suspicious detail was that in addition to being burned, the deceased Bohman also had a clean hole in his forehead. Did a tiny projectile from the explosion do this, or was it possible that he had been shot?

According to newspaper reports of the time, the wound was eventually identified as that of a bullet-hole. And as to

Robinson, though sometimes inaccurately reported as being in the train car with Bohman, which would make his survival miraculous, the fireman was only supposed to be in the engine room with him. As Robinson explained it to the press, the last thing he remembered was rolling a cigarette when they were stopped near the Toronto flag station. Considering he had a gash on the back of his head, it seemed likely someone knocked him out and then tossed him from the train, possibly while it was moving.

Remains of the engine with train cars behind it relatively unaffected. [Terrell County Memorial Museum]

That a saboteur was at work was backed by the train's brakeman, Earl Stirman, who reported to the *Bisbee Daily Review* of July 9, 1921, that he had seen "a 'tall slender man in black' run from the train and make off across the mountain a moment before the explosion occurred..." The article reports that Texas Rangers were currently searching for the mystery Man in Black and continued that, "Robinson told the coroner both he and the engineer had noticed a man riding a few cars back from the engine. Thinking he was a tramp stealing a ride they paid little attention to the man..."

Though officials puzzled over the motive of the crime, they at least suspected that it was done by someone familiar with the workings of a boiler room and a locomotive engine. "...the injectors, which supply water to the boiler, had been cut off," the papers explained.

And the story gets stranger still. Robinson committed suicide, shooting himself in the head, shortly before a hearing was held on the incident ten days after it had occurred. While this may point to his being a part of a conspiracy, others say that Robinson had suffered severe head trauma due to the incident. As it was, he had swelling of the brain which some speculate affected his mental state and led to his taking his own life. However, it's also possible that a conspirator involved in the incident only made it look like a suicide perhaps.

In his article on the incident, "The Paisano Pass Train Mystery" for *weekinweird.com*, Ken Summers observed that, "Strangely enough, that first recorded sighting [of the Marfa Lights] by cowhand Robert Reed Ellison was driving a herd through Paisano Pass when he saw the flickering lights in the sky." Summers goes on to note the coincidence of a Man in Black involved in the sabotage in an area associated with UFOs.

To this day, no one has been able to determine who would sabotage the engine or why. As for the lights in the sky, they are merely tangential and had nothing to do with the story even though Men in Black are associated with UFOs.

Photo of the Marfa Lights by Noe Torres.

17

THE HAUNTED
RAILROAD STATION

JUNE 1873
ST. PAUL, MINNESOTA

Stories of haunted locomotives and strange apparitions on railroad tracks are plenty, but tales of haunted railroad stations are less common. In October 25, 1872, the *Saint Paul Pioneer* newspaper reported that one of the train stations in the Saint Paul area had become essentially uninhabitable due to violent interactions between several ghostly figures and anyone who approached the station.

The story began in March 1872 with the collision of two trains belonging to the St. Paul & Pacific Railroad, which occurred at Randall station, 37 miles west of Willmar, Minnesota. A railroad worker named Connelly was killed, and several other persons injured. It was later said that Connelly's ghost haunted the Randall station, eventually driving out anybody who tried to occupy it.

In the original story, the dead man, Connelly, was described as the foreman of Randall station, although a dispute about his actual role arose later. In any event, following his death, another railroad worker was assigned to Randall as a replacement for him. The new foreman, whose name by coincidence was also Connelly, was described as "a sober industrious man, intelligent and always to be trusted, the last man who would be suspected of ignorant superstition or of an attempt to deceive."

It was after the new foreman took over that the ghostly manifestations began at the station. The January 9, 1873 edition of the *Minneapolis Star Tribune* reported, "He had not been long in charge when strange noises were heard; apparitions were seen at his bedside, sometimes entreating, then threatening as if in anger and bent on revenge. Several times Connelly [the new foreman] was said to have been thrown from his bed with violence, and it was said that his arms and several portions of his body bore evidence of rough handling. The imprint of hands and finger-nails were said to be visible, which he declared were made by his ghostly visitor."

Randall Train Station, circa 1902.

The *Saint Paul Pioneer* also described these and other strange occurrences at the haunted station: "Alarming incidents of this character occurred so frequently that Connelly finally asked to be removed from the division or from the house... The proceedings have continued up to the present time, and ... the people living in that part will go around the house for five miles rather than pass it. The spirit, or whatever it may be, is now seen about the house day and night. The doors of the house open and shut at night with an exceeding clatter. The phantasm of the approaching train is seen at night which, when it reaches the station, melts into thin air with the sound of a great tumult of voices and the cries of dying men. A lantern is also visible at intervals bobbing up and down along the road, but, belated travelers upon the prairie, when, they approach it, discover that it recedes from them and that they have been misled for miles."

The *Pioneer* also noted, "Tumults as of a great company dancing together are heard in the house, and outside a rushing noise as of a scurrying drove of cattle salutes the ear. The haunted place is avoided as far as possible by all, and three families which have endeavored to live therein within a short time have been frightened away."

Things finally came to a head on a day when the new foreman and several of his men were at supper when the door opened noiselessly, and there stood before them in the open door the ghostly form of the dead Connelly. The ghost was making menacing gestures at the men before it "disappeared by melting into space, and was seen no more."

An investigation into the story was made by the *Minneapolis Star Tribune*, published January 9, 1873, finding a number of errors with the story, as well as many exaggerations. The investigation did confirm the general facts, such as the train collision near Randall station in March 1872 and the death of a railroad worker named Connelly. However, they found that

Connelly was a "section hand" and not a "foreman" as claimed in the original story. Also, the ghostly apparition was seen by the brother of the dead man, not by the foreman who supposedly replaced him. The newspaper also suggested that the ghostly apparition may have been a "prank" perpetrated against the dead man's brother by some of the other railroad workers.

A Railroad Ghost—Depopulation of a Minnesota Railroad Station.

THE St. Paul *Pioneer* says: "We report only what we have heard," it says, "but the stories which have reached us are so well authenticated and are repeated by so many persons who are not inclined to superstitious notions that we are at a loss to give any opinion on the matter." It seems that the section foreman of the road at the locality named was formerly a man named Connelly, who is said to have taken great interest in his division. In March, 1872, a terrible accident occurred on the road at this station during a snow storm, whereby many lives were lost, including that of Connelly. This man was succeeded in his duties by a man also named Connelly, who occupied the station house as his predecessor had done before him. After he had been on duty for some months he suddenly became the victim of serious ghostly visitations and manifestations. The apparition of the dead foreman appeared nightly at his bed-side, wringing its hands apparently in entreaty and sometimes as if in anger. He had also been thrown violently out of his bed, and when he recovered himself he would find bruises and the imprints of fingers and hands upon his body. Alarming incidents of this character occurred so frequently that Connelly finally asked to be removed from the division or from the house. These particulars and many other details connected with the appearance of the phantom to other eyes were published at the time of their occurrence. The *Pioneer* now says that the proceedings have continued up to the present time, and that the people living in that part will go around the house for five miles rather than pass it. The spirit, or whatever it may be, is now seen about the house day and night. The doors of the house open and shut at night with an exceeding clatter. The phantasm of the approaching train is seen at night which, when it reaches the station, melts into thin air with the sound of a great tumult of voices and the cries of dying men. A lantern is also visible at intervals bobbing up and down along the road, but belated travelers upon the prairie, when they approach it, discover that it recedes from them and that they have been misled for miles. Tumults as of a great company dancing together are heard in the house, and outside a rushing noise as of a scurrying drove of cattle salutes the ear. The haunted place is avoided as far as possible by all, and three families which have endeavored to live therein within a short time have been frightened away. There are probably natural causes to account for most of these strange proceedings, but the fright of the people near the station house is none the less.

Portsmouth (Ohio) Times, 6-14-1873, p. 1.

18

SNAKE VERSUS TRAIN

1882
DOS PALMAS, CALIFORNIA

Back in the Golden Age of newspapers, many papers had an ornery habit of placing satirical, made-up stories alongside real ones, in order to increase readership. Readers in the know would get that the pieces were purely fictitious and for their amusement, while the more naïve crowd might believe them to be the unvarnished truth, no matter how incredible the story might seem. Perhaps the best example of these were "Snaik" stories, with snake purposefully being misspelled "snaik." As it was, newspaper readers were fascinated with stories about snakes, whether they were big or small. More often than not, the stories entailed giant snakes, a few of them might even have been true. Then there were stories about flying snakes and snakes with wings. The fantastic tale about to unfold told of a giant flying snake chasing a train.

The story originated in the *Los Angeles Times* and ran in numerous papers across the country throughout the winter of 1882. "One of the most startling stories that has been told in these parts for some time was related by the engineer and fireman who came in last night on the Southern Pacific express, and was corroborated by the passengers," began the crazy story. The train had just passed Dos Palmas, near Riverside, California, when the engineer noticed what looked like a column of sand moving very slowly from east to west about half a mile ahead.

THE WORST SNAKE STORY.

One of the most startling snake stories that has been told in these parts for some time was related by the engineer and fireman who came in last night on the Southern Pacific Express, and was corroborated by the passengers. It seems that just after the train had passed Dos Palms, the engineer noticed, about half a mile ahead, what looked like a column of sand moving very slowly from east to west. At that time it was only a short distance from the track, and moving at such a pace that it was evident that train and column would come together. When the two monsters were but a short distance apart it was discovered that the column was not sand, but an animal of some kind. It was moving in almost a perpendicular position, the tail dragging on the ground, and propelled by two large wings near the head. The bird, snake, or whatever it was, seemed to be about 30 feet long, and 12 inches in diameter. By this time everybody, almost, on the train, had put their heads out of the windows, and were hanging on the platform to get a look at the monster snake. The train and snake came together, but the snake's tail was not where it should have been, and a portion of his lower extremities was clipped off. This seemed to put this flying snake on his metal and he prepared for war. He wheeled around and gave chase to the flying train. The motion of the animal seemed to change in an instant, and he seemed to fly through the air two miles faster than chain lightning. In a few moments, he, she, or it, overtook the train and began war after the latest snake style. The angry animal kept over the train and gave the train a lively thrashing, roaring like a cow in distress all the time. After breaking several windows and frightening the women and children almost to death, the monster sailed off, followed by a shower of lead from the pistols of the passengers, which seemed to have no effect at all, if any of the bullets hit him. This is vouched for by every one who was on the train, and is given for what it is worth.

Buffalo Courier Express of February 3, 1882.

The strange formation was only a short distance from the track, "and moving at such a pace that it was evident that train and column would come together." As the distance closed between the train and the sand column, the engineer could see that it "was not sand, but an animal of some kind." The engineer claimed that the creature "was moving in almost a perpendicular position, the tail dragging on the ground, and propelled by two large wings near the head." The creature was some kind of winged snake over thirty feet long and twelve inches in diameter!

A FLYING SNAKE.

The Kind of Creature Conjured Up After Indulgence in Los Angeles Liquor.

Brooklyn Eagle of February 12, 1882.

By then, the passengers spotted the beast as well and were peering out of the windows and "hanging on the platform to get a look at the monster snake." Dramatically, the train and snake collided, and the snake's tail, or "a portion of his lower extremities" was clipped off. In the words of the paper, "This seemed to put this flying snake on his mettle, and he prepared for war." The enraged monster "wheeled around and gave chase to the train."

"The motion of the animal seemed to change in an instant, and he seemed to fly through the air two miles faster than chain lightning," the paper said. Within moments, the monster overtook the train and attacked: "The angry animal kept over the train and gave the train a lively thrashing, roaring like a cow in distress all the time. After breaking several windows and frightening the women and children almost to death, the monster sailed off, followed by a shower of lead from the pistols of the passengers, which seemed to have no effect at all, if any of the bullets hit him. This is vouched for by everyone who was on the train, and is given for what it is worth."

While both giant snakes and even flying snakes have their place in the realm of cryptozoology, the study of mystery animals like Bigfoot, this story was almost certainly made up by bored newspapermen with nothing else to report. The writers figured if stories about giant snakes were popular, then why not one about such a creature attacking a train? Notably the *Buffalo Courier Express* of February 3, 1882 called it "The Worst Snake Story." While it was certainly the most unbelievable, as far as "Snaik Stories" went, it was quite entertaining.

Artistic Conception.

19

THE FIREMAN WHO WOULD NOT DIE

DECEMBER 1879
LAFAYETTE, INDIANA

In railroad terms, a "fireman" is the person who maintained the locomotive's firebox, ensuring a constant and controlled burn of coal to generate the steam required for propulsion. Being so close to the firebox and boiler of the steam engine made being a fireman a very dangerous job. Unfortunately, firemen often had short careers and short lives. In 1879, following the death of a particular fireman, the railroad workers around Lafayette, Indiana, claimed to have seen his ghost on board the locomotive where he formerly worked.

The fireman in question was a man named Charles Johnson, 24, who worked for the Louisville, New Albany, and Chicago Railroad. The *Cincinnati (Ohio) Enquirer* said, "He was a man with a remarkably fine physique, and his manners were kind and attractive. He had a host of friends, and all the boys had a kind word and a warm place 'in their hearts' for Charley. He lived in Michigan City, and his run with engineer Henry Bishop was between that city and Lafayette."

On the morning of October 19, 1879, a very unfortunate accident befell Johnson, while carrying out his duties as a fireman for Engine No. 5 of the Louisville, New Albany, and Chicago Railroad. The tragedy happened as the locomotive was located on the tracks near Battle Ground, Indiana, the first station north of Lafayette. A report in the Lafayette newspaper said, "The deceased was a fireman and while in the act of shoveling coal into the engine, the coupling between the engine and tender gave way and the unfortunate man fell to the track and was instantly killed, both his legs and arms being crushed to atoms, three cars having passed over the body before the train could be stopped."

The *Cincinnati Enquirer* said, "Just as Charley was in the act of placing some coal into the furnace, and was standing upon the board between the locomotive and tender, the bolt broke, the engine, relieved of the great weight it had been striving to pull, shot ahead, and poor Charley Johnson fell between the tender and the engine. The fine form was horribly cut and mangled. His soul, without a moment's warning, had been cast into eternity."

The local people and co-workers had begun to forget about this great tragedy when suddenly something very unexpected and unsettling happened. On December 19, two months after

Johnson's demise, his ghostly form is said to have appeared aboard the same locomotive where he had perished. Henry Bishop, the engineer that was present in the train's cab when Johnson died, saw the specter with his own eyes. "Last night as he passed the point where the fatal accident occurred, suddenly, while his mind was upon another subject, there appeared to him at the window of his cab his late fireman. He passed through, smiled at Bishop, and the lips moved so that the teeth were distinctly visible. The form was distinct at first, but became luminous, and passed down between the engine and tender, and out of view. Bishop's fireman did not see the apparition, but Bishop is clearly satisfied that the spirit, the form, or the ghost of Johnson came in as he described. He seems greatly prostrated, and is reported to have declared his intention never to again make that run. He is an old engineer, and not likely to be terrified unless there is excellent reason. His present physical condition is a guarantee that he is greatly affected by the strange occurrence of last night."

STRANGE SPECTER.

A Phantom Fireman On the Road.

What an Engineer Who Runs Between Michigan City and Lafayette Saw, and the Apparition That Appeared Four Times in Michigan City—— A Strange Story.

SPECIAL DISPATCH TO THE EXAMINER.

LAFAYETTE, IND., December 18.—A thrilling, wild and startling story that reminds one of olden tales is passing from mouth to mouth to-day among employes of the Louisville, New Albany and Chicago Railroad. At first impression this morning when the writer heard the report it seemed as though some imaginative brain that wished to play upon the superstitious was responsible for the story, but prompted by a desire to investigate and determine the truth or falsity of the rumor he wended his way toward the depot of the road, and this is the result.

Six months ago there was employed upon this road, in the capacity of fireman, a robust, personable man, named Charles Johnson. He was a man with a remarkably fine physique, and his manners were kind and attractive. He had a host of friends, and all the boys had a kind word and a warm place "in their hearts" for Charley. He lived in Michigan City, and his run with engineer Henry Bishop was between that city and Lafayette. One night, when their train was at a point near Battle Ground, the first station on the road north of Lafayette, and just as Charley was in the act of placing some coal into the furnace, and was standing upon the board between the locomotive and tender, the bolt broke, the engine, relieved of the great weight it had been striving to pull, shot ahead, and poor Charley Johnson fell between

the tender and the engine. The fine form was horribly cut and mangled. His soul, without a moment's warning, had been cast into eternity. The remains were conveyed to Michigan City for burial, and people had for days ceased to think of the fatal accident. It had passed from their minds until last night and to-day it has been revived by a peculiar circumstance. It was rumored this morning that "Engineer Bishop had during his run last night seen the ghost of Charley Johnson." To such a report the intelligent, being naturally given no credence, but there are some very strange phases in the matter that we are bound to respect. Although Engineer Bishop very suddenly departed this morning for his home in Michigan City, the story he tells has been obtained by the EXAMINER, for the engineer repeated it to a number, and, coupled with other points as developed in Michigan City, it certainly deserves to receive respectful consideration.

Last night as he passed the point where the fatal accident occurred, suddenly——while his mind was upon another subject——there appeared to him at the window of his cab his late fireman. He passed through, smiled at Bishop, and the lips moved so that the teeth were distinctly visible. The form was distinct at first, but became luminous, and passed down between the engine and tender, and out of view. Bishop's fireman did not see the apparition, but Bishop is clearly satisfied that the spirit, the form, or the ghost of Johnson came in as he described. He seems greatly prostrated, and is reported to have declared his intention never to again make that run. He is an old engineer, and not likely to be terrified unless there is excellent reason. His present physical condition is a guarantee that he is greatly affected by the strange occurrence of last night.

Persons who profess to know, and who are certainly responsible and reliable, state that the phantom of Johnson has appeared to his family in Michigan City on four different occasions, and that they have been nearly frightened out of their wits by the unnatural visit of their dead relative.

While it is generally acknowledged that railroad men are superstitious, yet there are many who do not throw discredit upon Bishop's story. He has been free to talk about it, but the railroad men, his immediate acquaintances, are very reticent. There is an air of mystery about them, and the subject seems to be one that they would prefer not to discuss, although it is evident it greatly affects them.

The Cincinnati (Ohio) Enquirer, Dec. 19, 1879, p. 2.

It further developed that other witnesses in the area claimed they saw the same apparition. The *Cincinnati Enquirer* reported, "Persons who profess to know, and who are certainly responsible and reliable, state that the phantom of Johnson has appeared to his family in Michigan City on four different occasions and that they had been nearly frightened out of their wits by the unnatural visit of their dead relative. While it is generally acknowledged that railroad men are superstitious, yet there are many who do not throw discredit upon Bishop's story. He has been free to talk about it, but the railroad men, his immediate acquaintances, are very reticent. There is an air of mystery about them, and the subject seems to be one that they would prefer not to discuss, although it is evident it greatly affects them."

20

STRANGE TWISTS
OF FATE

1870s
IOWA AND NEW YORK

In the 1870s, railroad men in Iowa told the story of a local cattleman who mounted a one-man war against the railroad that laid tracks adjacent to his property. His anger and disdain toward the railroad caused the deaths of many innocent people and resulted in him suffering a bizarre twist of fate.

As the story goes, the wealthy cattleman refused to put up a fence to keep his cattle contained, and therefore, cattle would wander out from his land and onto the adjacent railroad tracks. On several occasions, passing trains would strike and kill the cattle, causing the cattleman great anger against the railroad company.

He tried suing the railroad, but his court cases were unsuccessful, with the judge admonishing him for not fencing his property to keep his cattle safe. This further intensified his bitter feelings toward the railroad.

Things finally came to a head when the cattleman apparently tried to take justice into his own hands. It seems he decided to sabotage the railroad tracks near his property by tying a loose rail across the top of the tracks.

When the first locomotive came along the tracks, it encountered the obstacle and was subsequently wrecked. Many persons were killed. After the accident, the bodies were taken to a nearby town, where all those killed were identified, except for one elderly woman, whose identity remained a mystery.

The wealthy cattleman waited a couple of days before going into town to collect his mail at the post office. He had heard that only one body from the train wreck remained in town – that of the elderly woman who had not yet been identified. As he read through his mail, he found a letter from his sister informing him that she was coming from the East by train to spend some time with him. Suddenly, an expression of horror spread across his face, and he rushed over to the town morgue.

Just as he had suspected, the body of the unidentified woman from the train wreck was that of his own sister. A newspaper account in the *New York Sun* said, "He rushed to the morgue and identified the body of the unknown lady as that of this sister."

Shortly after this happened, the cattleman's mental health deteriorated, and he eventually was judged to be insane. As his mental faculties declined rapidly, he was often heard ranting about the episode that led to the death of his beloved sister. In his ravings, he admitted that it was he who sabotaged the railroad tracks and caused the train carrying his sister to become wrecked, thereby killing her. Obviously, fate had taken a bizarre form of justice against the cattleman for bringing about the deaths of many innocent passengers on the train that he caused to wreck.

> A brakeman told a queer yarn about a wealthy old miscreant in Iowa, a farmer who did not fence his land properly, yet grumbled when his cattle were killed. The railroad beat him in the courts, and he treasured up the hardest feelings against the company. One day a rail was tied across the track near the old farmer's land, and the first passenger train that came along was wrecked. It was believed at the time that the farmer had tied the rail to the track. Many persons were killed, and all the bodies but that of an aged woman were identified. The first day after the accident the old farmer did not go to the town wherein this body awaited burial, but on the following morning he visited the Post Office, and received word that his sister was coming on from the East to visit him. He rushed to the morgue and identified the body of the unknown lady as that of this sister. In less than a year he became a maniac, and in his ravings admitted that he had wrecked the train.

New York Sun of July 29, 1879, p. 4.

In yet another tale with a strange twist of fate, the story is told of a train engineer in the Hudson River whose locomotive killed a blind man as he was attempting to cross the tracks. As the victim stepped right out in front of the moving engine, the engineer vividly saw the man's face. He saw an expression of great terror, saw the man raise his arms over his head wildly, and heard a horrible, piercing scream that was fully audible even above the loud pounding of the train engine.

The image of the blind man being struck and crushed under the locomotive became engraved in the engineer's brain, and it haunted him from that point onward. Every night, as the engineer passed the spot where the accident had happened, he saw the scene reenacted right before his eyes, as some sort of ghostly apparition. Greatly disturbed, he asked the railroad to work in the daytime instead of at night. But the horrible manifestation appeared to him even in the daytime!

Completely unnerved, he quit his job and took employment with another railroad company. "Yet at unexpected moments, the specter of the blind man seemed to start up in the track, to throw his arms over his head wildly, to scream, and to be crushed under the locomotive. It was more than the engineer could bear."

Finally, the strange twist of fate caught up to him, and he quit the profession altogether.

A story was told of a Hudson River engineer who killed a man that suddenly stepped in front of his engine. He had been watching the man and saw his face as he crossed over the track and walked into the engine. The man was blind. The engineer caught a glimpse of the victim's face as he was struck. His expression was one of terror. His scream was heard above the pounding of the engine. The sight haunted the engineer until he quit the business. Every night at that spot that scene was re-enacted. He took a day train, but at noon the apparition haunted the spot. He even went into the service of another company, yet at unexpected moments the spectre of the blind man seemed to start up in the track, to throw his arms over his head wildly, to scream, and to be crushed under the locomotive. It was more than the engineer could bear.

New York Sun of July 29, 1879, p. 4.

21

GROOM OF
LA LLORONA

1910s
TEXAS-MEXICO BORDER

Any story that can combine the likes of La Llorona, Pancho Villa, and the Mexican Revolution is obviously a winner. And lucky for us, it also included some haunted railroad tracks. Before going any further, for those unaware, La Llorona is a ghost sometimes also known as the Wailing Woman. Her legend spans the entire Southwest and even beyond in a few cases. The basis of her story is always the same in that it involves a mother who kills her own children. Usually, the mother is also a jilted lover who's been abandoned by the father of her children. After the woman kills her children, usually by drowning them, she immediately regrets what she's done and takes her own life. Thereafter she appears as the Wailing Woman, La Llorona, walking along the riverbeds crying out for her dead children. Her legend is especially prevalent in Mexico and also in New Mexico. As such, the story also bled into Texas.

Every town and village has its own unique origin story for La Llorona, but the one for the little town of San Benito, between Brownsville and Harlingen, is especially unique. It took place during the Mexican Revolution and, like many other La Llorona accounts, it had a well-to-do husband abandoning his wife and children, albeit with a twist. The burgeoning wailing woman was Dafne Bautista, the eldest daughter of a large family. Dafne's mother died giving birth to the family's sixth child, leaving the teenaged Dafne to take on the role of mother to her siblings. To help get by, she became a laundress like several other La Lloronas before her. She did her washing on the banks of the Resaca de los Fresnos, an oxbow lake.

Postcard of San Benito, TX.

There, she met her handsome suitor in the form of a Texas Ranger, Lawrence Woods, stationed in the area due to the encroaching tensions of the revolution. The two began a romance, and all in Dafne's family supported the notion of the couple being wed but one: Dafne's fifteen-year-old brother, Ovidio. To him, the Mexican guerillas of Pancho Villa were heroes and Texas Rangers were the enemy. Two years later, Dafne and Lawrence were married and had two infant sons. Dafne still worked as a laundress and often fretted over both Ovidio, who had fled to fight with Villa's men, and Lawrence, still in the Texas Rangers.

The inevitable tragedy struck when Ovidio and a group of revolutionaries were killed by Texas Rangers, Lawrence among them. It was too much for the couple to bear, and Lawrence left Dafne and his two sons behind to return to Houston, where his mother resided. Despite Lawrence's promises to send money to her and the boys, Dafne was understandably distraught at the tragedy that had befallen them all. Calmly, Dafne collected her two boys, telling them that she had to do some laundry at the lake. She loaded them onto a burro as she had done so many times before and set off for the lake. There, she told the boys they would take a swim before she did her work. Taking both of them into her arms, she waded into the depths until their heads were under the water and drowned them. Then, Dafne swam out into the deepest part of the lake and let herself drown.

The waterways of San Benito as depicted on a vintage postcard.

About to board the train, Lawrence had a premonition that something awful was about to happen. He rushed to the lake, knowing there his wife would be. Instead, he saw only the dead bodies of his boys floating in the water. Dafne was nowhere to be found. Lawrence took to heavy drinking and was eventually hit by a train as he wandered along some railroad tracks one night. That was only the beginning of the story, though. Sometime later, Dafne's younger sisters took over her laundry business and began to frequent the lake themselves. One night, the youngest sibling was walking along the shores when she saw her dead sister emerge from the water, wailing and crying, "Where are my children!?"

Dafne, either not recognizing her youngest sister, or perhaps not caring, seized her with her long fingernails and dragged her beneath the waves to her doom. The other girls would eventually follow, and thus began La Llorona's reign of terror at San Benito. Likewise, even Lawrence's ghost stalked the railroad tracks, making this one of the few instances where La Llorona's husband got in on the hauntings as well.

22

THE HEADLESS FIREMAN

1890s
ILLINOIS

Employment on the early locomotives was neither pleasant nor safe. Terrible accidents were common, and often the victims of these accidents were horribly disfigured or dismembered. In the 1890s, railroad men in Illinois told the story of a particular tragedy and the haunting that followed it.

As reported by the *Magnolia (Mississippi) Gazette* in its November 12, 1892 edition, veteran train engineer Henry E. Archer related a harrowing tale about a "Jonah," which is the name given by railroad men to locomotives that are considered to be cursed or haunted. "Locomotive engineers are not, perhaps, more superstitious than other people, but I have known more than one to throw up his position rather than take out an engine that was regarded as unlucky."

Archer then related an incident that he said happened some years earlier on board a train belonging to the Illinois Central Railroad, where Archer had worked for 20 years.

According to Archer, the steam engine exploded on the tracks, hurling large pieces of metal in all directions. One chunk of iron neatly severed the head of the train's fireman. The horrible tragedy notwithstanding, the engine was eventually rebuilt and "made good as new."

However, in the estimation of the railroad veterans, this engine was now considered a "Jonah," and there was great hesitancy to work on it. "No engineer could be found to run it more than one trip. It was soon whispered about that it was haunted; that the headless fireman had an unpleasant habit of appearing on the tender with pick and shovel and insisting on firing up."

Illinois Central Locomotive Pulls Up to Station, Circa 1890

A HAUNTED LOCOMOTIVE

"There are on nearly every railroad locomotives that are known as "Jonahs," said Henry E. Archer, who has spent twenty years in the service of the Illinois Central, and is at present sojourning at the Southern. "Locomotive engineers are not, perhaps, more superstitious than other people, but I have known more than one to throw up his position rather than take out an engine that was regarded as unlucky. Some years ago an engine on an Illinois road blew up, cutting the fireman's head off with a segment of boiler iron. The engine was rebuilt and made as good as new, but no engineer could be found to run it more than one trip. It was soon whispered about that it was haunted; that the headless fireman had an unpleasant habit of appearing on the tender with pick and shovel and insisting on firing up. One night an engineer and his fireman deserted the locomotive while out on a run and the conductor attempted to bring the train in. He was not afraid of ghosts! not he! But he sidetracked at the first opportunity and waited until daylight before completing the run. He told me that the ghost was no joke; that every time the furnace door was thrown open the headless apparition entered the cab bearing a shadowy scoop of coal. For a month the engine lay in the shop. Then an engineer, who was compelled to either take it out or lose his position, mounted it. Before he had run a dozen miles it went through a culvert, wrecked the train and killed nine people. It was never rebuilt."

Magnolia (Mississippi) Gazette of November 12, 1892, p.1.

The headless apparition created havoc with train crews, including one instance where both the engineer and the fireman, when confronted by the ghost during a night run, jumped off the train, abandoning their stations. The train's conductor, who claimed not to believe in ghosts, stepped in and took over the train's controls. The conductor managed to pull the train off the main tracks onto a siding, where he waited until daylight before completing the journey to the next station.

Upon arriving at the station, the conductor seemed to no longer be a skeptic regarding ghosts. "He told me that the ghost was no joke," Archer said, "That every time the furnace door was thrown open, the headless apparition entered the cab, bearing a shadowy scoop of coal."

It was said that the locomotive was taken out of service after this incident for about a month, with the company not able to find an engineer to agree to take it out. Finally, a certain engineer was told that he either agreed to take the engine out or he would be fired. He grudgingly agreed to take it on.

The locomotive had not gone more than twelve miles before it went through a culvert and wrecked, killing nine people. After that, it was never rebuilt.

[From the Springfield Republican.]

A Haunted Locomotive.

A locomotive that is possessed of a devil is the sensation at South Manchester, Connecticut. The engine is called the "Pioneer," formerly the "Canonchet," and belongs to the Hartford, Providence and Fishkill Railroad. She was sold to another road recently, but owing to some misunderstanding was never delivered, and to get her out of the way the company sent her from Hartford to South Manchester a week or two ago to be housed in the engine-house there. She behaved herself like any well bred engine the first two nights, but on the third the watchman heard strange noises issuing from all parts of her, noises unlike anything he ever heard before. This continued every night, and was heard by his brother, who came to keep him company in the uncanny place. Then the story got abroad that there was a haunted engine at the shop, and believers and unbelievers began to flock around. The noises continued to be audible. There was a rapping, now in the fire-box, now in the boiler, and anon in the smoke-stack, as though some person inside were striking the iron with a muffled stick, and a hollow and dismal reverberation followed each blow.

The most careful and thorough examination failed to disclose any trickery or the possibility of any, and the impudent spirits would keep up the racket even while the scrutiny was going on. People go to the engine house and stay nights to hear the manifestations, and it is related that one young man who was making unseemly jests about the ghosts suddenly grew deathly pale and fell in a swoon. When he recovered he said he saw a ghostly figure glide out of the engine and point its bony finger at him.

There are divers theories to account for the business. A gentleman from Pittsburg, who knows all about iron and locomotives, says it is the molecular action of the iron striving to return from the artificial fibrous state, as seen in wrought iron, to the granulated, or pig-iron state. The believers in the spirit theory floor him at once, however, by asking why the noises are loudests on alternate nights, and why they always occur between 9 o'clock, p. m. and 5, a. m.

Marshall Saline County (Missouri) Progress, 12-3-1873, p. 1

23

GHOSTLY TOURIST ATTRACTION

In the 19th century, people often flocked to places where mysterious "rapping" was heard, typically in houses and other buildings, as well as from walls and furniture. Spiritualists claimed to be able to communicate with the spirits of the dead by rapping on various surfaces and then getting a response back from the departed using the same rapping sounds. This craze, known as "Spirit Rapping," first broke out in the mid-1800s, and often occurred in association with a seance.

What was not typical, however, was for rapping and other unexplained sounds to be heard from inside a locomotive while it was parked inside an engine house. This is exactly what happened in late November 1873 in South Manchester, Connecticut. Hundreds of spectators traveled from miles around to witness the strange noises that emanated from the innards of one particular locomotive.

Owned by the Hartford, Providence, and Fishkill Railroad, the locomotive was named "Pioneer" and had been recently transferred from Hartford, Connecticut, to South Manchester. About three days after being placed inside an engine house there, the night watchman reported hearing strange sounds issuing from "all parts of her." He said the noises were "unlike anything he had ever heard before."

A typical séance.

On every subsequent night, the strange concert of noises was heard coming from the locomotive. The watchman's brother showed up one night to keep him company, and he too experienced the phenomenon. Soon, people found out about the noises and began flocking into the engine house every evening to hear for themselves.

"There was a rapping, now in the fire-box, now in the boiler, and anon in the smoke stack, as though some person inside were striking the iron with a muffled stick, and a hollow and dismal reverberation followed each blow."

Railroad company personnel were called in to thoroughly examine the locomotive and its inner workings. They carefully and thoroughly looked at it, noting that the sounds continued even while they were in the process of carrying out their investigation. In the end, the experts concluded that the cause remained unknown, and that it was no prank or trickery.

The reputation of the locomotive grew, and more spectators showed up to gawk. "People go to the engine house and stay nights to hear the manifestations." In one particular case, a young man was joking about the ghosts when he suddenly grew deathly pale and fell unconscious. Upon reviving, he said he saw a ghostly figure glide out of the locomotive and point a bony finger at him.

Terror on the Train!

A typical engine house of the period.

Artist's depiction of investigation into rapping.

The strange phenomenon was not without its skeptics. A railroad expert from Pittsburgh, Pennsylvania, claimed that the noises were caused by a settling of the metals that were used in the manufacturing process, and the subsequent molecular action. But his theory was challenged by the "believers in the spirit theory," who pointed out that the noises were loudest on alternate nights and they always occurred between 9 p.m. and 5 a.m.

Apparently, the mystery of this ghostly tourist attraction was never solved. The historical record contains no further stories about it after 1873.

24

THE BOSTIAN BRIDGE HORROR

AUGUST 27, 1891
STATESVILLE, NORTH CAROLINA

Paranormal investigators have argued that hauntings tend to occur at the sites of sudden tragic events where many lives are snuffed out in an instant, leaving behind a "residual" psychic energy. A case in point is the site of one of the most deadly and tragic accidents in the early history of America's railroads – the August 27, 1891 crash of a Western North Carolina passenger train, killing 22 people, most of them instantly. Some of the passengers and crew were killed by trauma, while others drowned in the creek below. To this day, the site of this horrific crash remains etched in the minds of local residents. In the decades following the crash, a number of people have reported seeing spectral apparitions related to the train going over the same bridge.

But returning to 1891, Steam Locomotive No. 166 of train No. 9 of the Richmond & Danville Railroad left Statesville, North Carolina, at around 2:30 a.m. with a five-car train. The five cars comprised a baggage car, a first- and second-class car, a Pullman sleeper, and the railroad superintendent's private car. A total of 52 passengers were aboard the train at the time of the wreck.

The train pulled out of Statesville about 34 minutes late and was travelling at close to 40 miles per hour, a bit faster than normal in order to make up for the delay. Within five minutes after leaving the station, it approached the Bostian Bridge, a

70-foot-tall bridge that spanned Third Creek. The bridge, built of rock and brick, had five arches or spans and was about 200 feet long. It was undamaged in the crash. A local newspaper of the time said, "It is as safe as a bridge could be – in fact, a track on solid ground could be made no safer. Trains, therefore, do not slack speed upon approaching it."

Train No. 9, being run by engineer William West, came rumbling across the bridge without slowing down when it hit a problem in the rail. At first, it was suspected that the engine might have hit a "gap," a small intentional space left between two connecting rail sections, designed to allow for expansion and contraction due to temperature changes. (If the gap became too large due to poor maintenance, it would become a major safety risk.) However, later the gap theory was replaced by the idea that the rail was damaged deliberately by saboteurs.

THE SCENE AT THE MOMENT OF THE DISASTER.

(Courtesy Wikimedia.)

The *Charlotte (N.C.) Democrat* said, "The engine struck the gap, gave a great bound and fell down into the space. Along with it went every car in the train, one after the other, with their human loads, crashing upon the hard ground 90 feet below. Every car was smashed into kindling wood and the wreckage was heaped in a confused and disordered pile. Down under were the torn and mangled bodies of the crew and unfortunate passengers."

Of the 52 passengers aboard, 22 were killed, and only four walked away from the wreckage relatively uninjured. Some of the less injured survivors, including the conductor, walked back to Statesville to report the disaster. Rescue workers made their way to the train, and took the injured to Statesville, which did not have a hospital, so they needed to be accommodated and cared for in private homes. The dead were taken to a tobacco warehouse for identification.

Bostian Bridge Train Wreck. (Public Domain – Wikimedia)

The *Charlotte (N.C.) Democrat* reported, "The track for fully a half mile east of and across the bridge is down grade and perfectly straight. The approach to the bridge is upon a very heavy fill, and the train was no doubt moving at a very rapid rate, as the structure is of such a character as to be thought as solid as the earth itself. It is built of rock and brick, and has five arches or spans. It is perhaps 200 feet long."

"The embankments on either side are very abrupt, and the height from the ground at the center arch to the track level above is 70 feet.... The track, together with the cross ties, throughout the whole length of the bridge, were swept clear from the stringers and carried into the gorge with the wreck, but the bridge itself was left without a mark of damage upon it. The steel rails were twisted into every conceivable shape, and interwoven in the wreck in every direction."

Bostian Bridge train wreck. (Public Domain – Wikimedia)

An investigation into the cause of the crash speculated that an unknown group of "train wreckers" had deliberately sabotaged the railroad tracks. The *Charlotte (N.C.) Democrat* said, "In support of this, they say that the spikes and bolts which held the rails and crossties to the wooden stringers across the viaduct had been deliberately drawn by some person unknown, and the train thereby wrecked. To prove this, they will produce as evidence spikes, with marks upon them indicating that they had been freshly drawn, and bolts with the taps removed with no marks or breaks in the threads to indicate that it had been done by violence. These bolts and spikes, we understand, were found upon the top of the bridge...."

THE SCENE AT THE BRIDGE AFTER THE DISASTER.

(Courtesy Wikimedia)

The official coroner's inquest into the deaths at the train wreck determined that the train wreck was "caused by a loose rail, the bolts and spikes of the same having been taken out by some person or persons unknown to the jury, with tools or implements belonging to said railroad company, which said tools or implements were by gross negligence on the part of said railroad company left in an open shed accessible to every passerby." It further said, "We do also find that several of the cross ties at and near the break in the said railroad track, where said rail was displaced were unsound and should have been replaced, and that the superstructure on the bridge was in part defective, and further that the high rate of speed maintained in running trains over this bridge deserves and has the censure and condemnation of this jury."

Over the years, a number of theories about the cause surfaced, including that vagrants had set up a camp on the tracks and had damaged some of the rails. Later, when it was disclosed that the Richmond & Danville Railroad Company was in financial difficulties at the time of the wreck, some people felt the company may have wrecked the train to collect the insurance money or may have simply been negligent in maintaining the track.

Reports of ghostly happenings at the site of the crash surfaced rather quickly. In fact, on the first anniversary of the tragedy, a very strange incident happened to a group of people that were out for a walk in the area of the Bostian Bridge. They saw a man dressed in a railroad uniform approach them and ask them what time it was. His appearance seemed to match that of Hugh K. Linster, a baggage master who had been killed in the 1891 tragedy. After they gave him the time, he "vanished before the group's eyes," according to the *New Bern (N.C.) Sun Journal.*

As the decades passed, more reports began surfacing of people seeing ghostly figures and strange happening in the vicinity of the Bostian Bridge crash site. On August 27, 1941, on the 50th anniversary of the wreck, a strange incident happened to a married couple, Pat and Larry Hayes of Columbia, S.C. The story was told in the October 28, 2014 edition of the *Statesville (N.C.) Record and Landmark* by librarian Joel Reese of the Iredell County Public Library.

The couple were on a vacation road trip to the mountains of North Carolina. It was late at night when they approached the area of the Bostian Bridge. Larry was driving and pulling a camper, while Pat and the kids slept. Suddenly, one of their tires blew out, and the Hayes car began to veer. Larry managed to get the car off the road and park it. Not having a tire jack, he decided to leave his wife and kids with the vehicle while he walked the two miles to the nearest town, Statesville, to get help. It was a little past 2 a.m. What happened next was summarized by Reese:

"Sitting in the dark car, Pat heard the whistle of a train in the distance. She listened as the train got closer until she could make out the light of the engine. The train grew close as she watched it start across a nearby bridge. To her shock the train began to lurch on the tracks until it slid off the bridge falling into the dark chasm below.

"Pat sat stunned as she heard the sound of the train crashing. Jumping from the car she could hear people screaming and crying for help as she ran forward to look down. Below lay the train smashed into pieces of metal and wood. Staring in shock, she realized there was a man standing beside her. He was dressed in a railroad uniform and curiously asked her for the time.

> "After being sworn find from the testimony and our personal examination that the above named persons came to their death by the wrecking of the train on the Western North Carolina railroad at Bostian's Bridge, over Third Creek, in Iredell county, N. C., on Thursday morning Aug. 21, 1891. The said wrecking of the train being caused by a loose rail, the bolts and spikes of the same having been taken out by some person or persons un known to the jury, with tools or implements belonging to said railroad company which said tools or implement were by gross negligence on the part of said railroad company left in an open shed accessible to every passerby. We do also find that several of the cross ties at and near the break in the said railroad track, where said rail was displaced were unsound and should have been replaced, and that the superstruction on the bridge was in part defective, and further that the high rate of speed maintained in running trains over this bridge deserves and has the censure and condemnation of this jury.

Charlotte (N.C.) Democrat of September 4, 1891, p.2.

"Hearing a car door slam, she turned and saw her husband and another man emerging from a car. Running toward them she cried that there had been a terrible train wreck. The three ran back but the man was gone and when they looked below there was no sign of a train or wreckage."

"After daylight the couple came to Statesville and to their surprise, they learned that not only had there not been a train wreck, but the last train wreck in Iredell County had been exactly fifty years earlier at that same bridge on Aug. 27, 1891. When they asked about the railroad man, they learned that the train's baggage master, Hugh K. Linster, was killed in the accident."

On August 27, 1991, the 100th anniversary of the tragedy, about 400 people showed up and camped at the scene in a commemoration that had elements of a carnival. Vendors sold T-shirts, books, and other items to the attendees. "Conditions seemed almost perfect for the ghostly return of engine No. 9," said the *New Bern (N.C.) Sun Journal.* "The sky was overcast, just as it was when the ill-fated passenger train jumped the track and plunged off Bostian Bridge 100 years ago, killing nearly two dozen passengers. Darkness swallowed the storied trestle and the surrounding countryside. And the waters of Third Creek – although far more shallow than in 1891 – still ran beneath one of the bridge's majestic arches."

The 1991 gathering stated their desire to see the ghostly train reappear, but they were disappointed. "The train never came," the newspaper reported.

In 2010, another group gathered at the site on the 119th anniversary of the wreck, including about twelve amateur "ghost hunters." In the middle of festivities, suddenly a Norfolk Southern train rounded a bend in the tracks, catching the group off guard and causing them to scramble madly off the tracks. One of the attendees, Christopher Kaiser, pushed a woman aside at the last second to save her life, but he was struck by the train and thrown to the bottom of the 100-foot ravine beneath the trestle, where he was later pronounced dead.

It seems the Bostian Bridge Horror had claimed yet another victim. To this day, the site is still viewed with fear and awe by the inhabitants of the area. It remains one of the most notable paranormal sites related to trains in the United States.

25

THE PHANTOM TRAIN WRECK

LATE 1800s
PINE CITY, MINNESOTA

Pine City, located about 70 miles north of Minneapolis, is a quintessential Minnesota small town of about 3,000 people. Southeast of Pine City is the mysterious, and some say haunted, Devils Lake, which is a 16-acre body of extremely muddy, murky water that is believed to be about 80 feet deep. Some people say the eerie lake holds the remains of many secrets, including a train that derailed in the late 1800s, plunging into the lake never to be seen again. To this day, the train, including all its cars is believed to be at the bottom of the lake, waiting to be rediscovered.

Extensive research into the newspaper articles of the era have failed to find any articles about a train crash at Devils Lake; however, there is other evidence that supports the possibility of a train crash. The railroad tracks that passed close to the lake included a wooden railroad trestle allowing trains to pass over the south part of the lake. By the late 1800s, that trestle was considered to be in a poor state of repair, and people feared it could cause a train to fall into the lake. The March 15, 1889 edition of the *Pine County Pioneer* reported on these problems, as pointed out by researcher Ron T. Keagle on *PressPubs.com*.

"The article says that the trestle across the south end of Devils Lake is in very bad condition, and is almost impossible to maintain because the west shore of the lake seems to be sliding down into the water," Keagle wrote. The article he referenced also noted that the railroad track moved as much as six inches in a night. The article referred to the phenomenon as a 'perpetual land-slide,' and said that quite a distance to the west of the lake, there was a large crevice in the earth's surface that seemed to be a break from which the landslide started. It also said that "the railroad company should keep a watchman there night and day for the purpose of signaling trains in case the track is disrupted by the landslide."

But if a train went down into the lake at some point, wouldn't the railroad company have tried to recover it? Keagle said, "Because trains and locomotives were very heavy, they could be really hard to recover from these submersions in water and mire." As it was, it would have taken much time and labor to recover the train, and the cost of the effort would have exceeded the value of the train itself, so it made more sense to simply leave it. Therefore, it's not hard to believe that the train's owners let it stay put at the lake bottom.

But, people ask, why would there be no media coverage of a train wreck in Pine City? Keagle explained that many train wrecks went unreported in newspapers unless someone died, and further explained that "the physical loss of equipment was often accompanied by loss of the record of the physical loss, as may be the case with the Devils Lake legend."

The train is believed to have been a "special," thus not appearing in regular schedules or timetables. Also, the train was believed to have been of a specialized purpose, namely a "circus train," essentially a cargo train carrying caged animals, tents, and various types of equipment employed in a circus. It was likely crewed by two or three men, who might have easily jumped off the train when they saw the trestle collapsing beneath them.

Proponents of the circus train theory have said the train was headed north to Canada, for setup and performances there. When it was "lost," the company that owned it did not have sufficient financial resources or insurance coverage to attempt any sort of recovery or even an investigation. They just took the loss, possibly going out of business.

It is definitely possible that the train crew escaped the wreck. Train crews often jumped off the locomotive when they saw that a wreck was inevitable. Also, since the crew consisted of no local people, that would be another reason it would never have been reported in the local newspapers. "With a freight train, only two or three men would have been in the locomotive cab, and thus at immediate risk of death in a derailment," said Keagle. As it was, Pioneer-era freight trains, while slower than today's, shared a similar inability to stop rapidly; thus, jumping clear of a collision was a common survival tactic. To stay safe, one had to be constantly on the lookout for trouble. Numerous engineers and firemen escaped death by leaping from their locomotives before collisions, landslides, washed-out trestles, fires, or boulders stopped them. Therefore, the train may have derailed at Devils Lake and ended up in the water without loss of life if the engineer and fireman anticipated the derailment and escaped beforehand. "Or they may have ridden it into the lake and escaped the cab after the engine went into the water," Keagle said.

This leaves us with the incredible mystery of a train that plunged into Devils Lake and was never seen again. Keagle believes that the geology of the lake may have prevented any recovery of the fallen train: "In considering the idea of a train lost in Devils Lake, one naturally suspects that the substantial depth of the lake played a prominent role in the loss and inability to recover. With the technology of over a century ago, connecting lifting cables to a fifty-ton locomotive in ninety feet of water would have been nearly impossible. Depending on the nature of the lake bottom, the engine might have been buried in mud besides being ninety feet underwater."

The Murky Depths of Devils Lake. (Artist's Rendition)

Keagle pointed out that even if the train wreck occurred in a shallower part of the lake, it may have been buried under as much as 30 feet of mud. The fact that it may be buried under mud could also explain why scuba divers in modern times have seen no trace of it while exploring the murky depths of Devil's Lake.

So, if the story was never published, how did people eventually find out about this train wreck? Keagle said that in 1990 Pine City historian Anna Vach told him that she first heard the story from an old-time resident of Pine City who was living in town at the time of the crash and knew about it. In a letter to Keagle, the historian said, "They [the townspeople] heard the northbound coming, blowing the whistle, but it never came into Pine City. Upon investigation, they found only the land slide and train tracks leading into Devils Lake."

The unnamed "lady" who said she knew about the crash sent a letter to the Pine City Historical Society forty years after the wreck happened, which would have put the date of the letter between 1930 and 1940. In the letter, the lady mentioned that her grandfather also knew the story of the train that had fallen in the lake.

It appears that the story then rests upon the oral testimony of persons living in Pine City at the time of the supposed train wreck. However, this oral evidence seems to go along with the newspaper report from 1899 stating that the condition of the south trestle at Devils Lake was very poor and could cause a train to fall into the lake at any time.

Terror on the Train!

Over time, the story of this lost train seems to have been added onto. People began to say that the train was carrying some measure of wealth, perhaps in gold. It is uncertain, though, why a circus train that nobody even bothered to look for after it crashed would be suspected of carrying gold?

With the added angle of lost gold, the legend of the lost train had gone too far, according to Mike Gainor, editor of the *Pine County News*. In 2021, Gainor wrote, "It was brought to my attention that an area publication reprinted a portion of the Pine County *Wikipedia* page that addresses this lost train in Devils Lake story. But that page (and that publication) didn't stop at the story previously described, the story that has been circulating for decades in Pine City. No, the train in the *Wikipedia* article is now much more than an ordinary train – it's a circus train, full of Confederate gold, being smuggled to a zoo in Canada before it derailed into our own Devils Lake."

For Gainor, the "enhancement" of the story to include the smuggling of Confederate gold to Canada was just too much. Pointing out that most anyone can edit a *Wikipedia* page, Gainor wrote, "I think it's pretty clear that someone was having some fun here, and decided to amp the legend up to a new level of absurdity."

But the idea that the lost train may have been carrying treasure has lured treasure hunters to Devils Lake, hoping to locate the wreckage. As of the writing of this book, however, the solution to this baffling mystery remains elusive.

In December 2014, journalist Donna Heath of the *Pine City Pioneer* wrote, "A story that refuses to die in Pine City is the saga of Devil's Lake that a railroad train at one time sunk to the bottom. Vernon Hinze of Mora called the *Pioneer* office to tell the editor he dove in Devil's Lake about 20 years ago and found what might have been the corner of a boxcar. Only about three or four feet of metal were sticking out of the muck about 35-40 ft. under water. Vernon, who is Charlotte Hinze's son, said he believes the lake bottom is suspended like quicksand, with springs running through it."

The article continued that Vernon went to a depth of about 60 feet when he thought he had finally reached the bottom. He had with him a large underwater flashlight when he made the dive, and reached as far as he could into the muck until he could no longer see his hand.

"He never felt a solid bottom," the article concluded.

26

THE SERIAL KILLER WHO RODE TRAINS

1898 - 1912
MANY U.S. CITIES

By the late 1800s, rail transportation was clearly the best way to move cargo and people quickly and efficiently around the United States. This fact was not lost upon criminals, who sought to use trains for their own nefarious purposes, which brings us to the case of an axe murderer named Paul Mueller. He is believed to have "ridden the rails" throughout America, randomly seeking out and killing at least 59 people and possibly as many as 100, from 1898 to 1912. Most of the murders took place near railroad stations, which leads to the theory that Mueller used "freighthopping" to move around the country.

Mueller, believed to have worked as an itinerant lumberjack, was highly skilled with axes. Typically, he would commit his murders in small, remote towns with little or no law enforcement personnel. Upon arriving in a new town, he would seek out a nearby family farm. He would hide in the barn or other outbuilding and observe the family for a while, after which he would kill the adults while they slept and, if young girls were present, he would sexually assault them before killing them also.

Mueller is believed to have killed at least 14 entire families, consisting of a total of 59 persons. The murders occurred in Oregon, Kansas, Florida, Arkansas, and other locations. In addition, during the years in which Mueller was active, there were 25 other families murdered, consisting of 94 persons — which may or may not be linkable to Mueller.

The story of the serial killer who rode trains was first published in a 2017 book by Bill James and Rachel McCarthy James, titled *The Man from the Train: The Solving of a Century-Old Serial Killer Mystery*. Until the authors did their extensive historical research into numerous unsolved murders from 1898 to 1912, most of the cases were thought to be isolated, unlinked killings. Some of the killings were said to be the work of a murderer that was nicknamed "Billy the Axman."

According to *The Man from the Train*, the Mueller killings ended abruptly in 1912, at which time he may have been caught and incarcerated for a lesser offense — or something else may have happened to him, including possibly returning to his native Germany.

The start of his murderous activities seems to be traceable to the killing of Francis D. Newton and his family in Brookfield, Massachusetts on January 7, 1898, according to author Troy Taylor, who included their story in his 2012 book *Murdered in Their Beds*.

Francis D. Newton was a successful and well-respected farmer and cattleman who often hired farmhands to work with him. These men were mostly drifters, and in addition to paying them their salary, Newton gave them room and board on the family farm.

Sometime prior to 1898, Newton made the grave mistake of hiring Paul Mueller to work for him. Mueller, a native of Germany who spoke only broken English, had previously worked at a nearby country club, where he was known, and feared, for having a "hot temper." Upset at the owners of the country club, he walked off the job one day, after which he went and asked Newton to hire him as his farm hand. Newton agreed to hire him, being unaware of his bad reputation with the country club.

At first, Newton got along very well with his new man. Over the years, the farmer had learned how to handle his workers, having had many of them. As long as they did their work, he was agreeable toward them.

At some point, though, Newton complained to Mueller about his work, and Mueller's dark side was activated, unbeknownst to his boss. According to author Troy Taylor, the complaint might not have been a very serious one, but apparently Mueller took it very seriously.

Shortly thereafter, Newton's neighbors noticed that his farm seemed in neglect. The dairy cows had not been milked, and the cattle had not been fed. Neighbors searched the house, forced open the front door, found that the house had been ransacked, and found Francis, his wife, and daughter, all dead.

The January 11, 1898 edition of the *Boston Globe* reported that Mueller first killed his boss: "The body of Newton, clad in a night robe, lay on the bed with sheets and comforter piled on top of the crushed skull as if the assailant sought to be spared the sight of this work as he rifled the drawers of the bureau. The head was battered beyond recognition, and this had been the only target. The body lay on the right side as if the attack had been made while the victim slumbered, and nearby was an open pocket book, the lining of which had been pulled out by the nervous fingers of the man who was in such a hurry to possess himself of the contents."

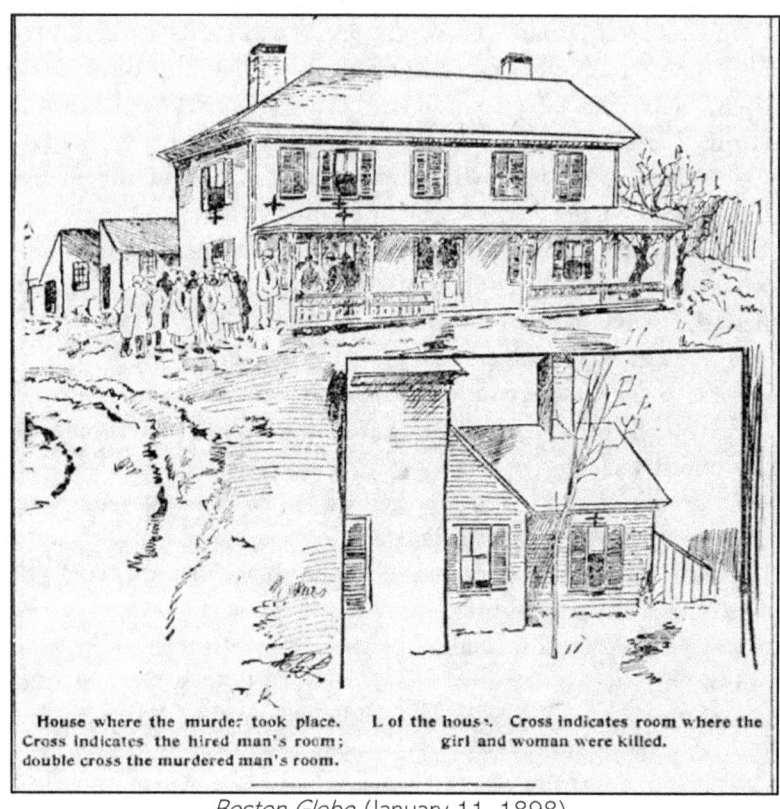

House where the murder took place.   L. of the house.   Cross indicates room where the
Cross indicates the hired man's room;   girl and woman were killed.
double cross the murdered man's room.

Boston Globe (January 11, 1898)

The *Globe* then reported on the horrible and tragic condition of the bodies of Newton's wife and stepdaughter: "The investigators came upon the bodies of the mother and the little adopted child, both even more ferociously mutilated than that of the man in the room above. The relentless fury of the murderer was not spent when the skulls had been crushed in several places" and he had also driven "his ax into the bodies of woman and child."

Terror on the Train!

"The autopsy held this afternoon ... showed that Mr. Newton had been struck four times on the left side of the head, the steel ax head penetrating to the brain in each instance; an additional blow on the cheek splintered the upper jaw."

Mr. Newton's Room, Where He Was Killed. Paul's Room the One Beyond.

Room Where Mrs Newton and Elsie Were Killed.

Boston Globe (January 11, 1898)

"Mrs. Newton and Ethel were struck five times on the head, just over the left temple, and each mark was distinct. Neither had been outraged [raped], nor did they appear to have been awakened, for the intruder had but one purpose, slaughter."

It was quickly suspected that the murderer had been Paul Mueller, who had disappeared from the farm immediately after the crime. The *Boston Globe* noted, "Paul Muller, or Miller, as he was sometimes called, a tramp sailor, carpenter, and farm hand, who had worked at the Newton place for the past two months, is suspected. Muller has been missing since Friday at midnight, when he was seen coming from the farm to the Brookfield railroad station.... If the identification of railroad men is correct, Muller went to New Haven on the night train Friday. He had ample time to catch this train from West Brookfield, two miles beyond the point where he was last seen, as it leaves West Brookfield at 1:20 a.m."

Author Troy Taylor added in his book *Murdered in Their Beds: The History & Hauntings of Villisca & The Midwest Ax Murders*, "According to the autopsy that followed, neither woman had been raped. All three had their skulls violently beaten and all were drugged with laudanum – an opiate of the era – before their deaths." Later, it was also discovered that all the horses on the farm had been poisoned. The killer next ransacked the house, taking all the cash he could get, along with coins belonging to Mr. Newton. Oddly, other valuable items, like the Newtons' gold watches, were left behind. Lastly, the killer set the house on fire with kerosene in an effort to hide the evidence. However, the fire went out before it could effectively cover his tracks.

Boston Globe (January 11, 1898)

It is believed by the authors of *The Man from the Train: The Solving of a Century-Old Serial Killer Mystery* that the murder of the Newton family was the start of Mueller's murderous career. Using trains as a convenient means of traveling quickly between geographically separated destinations, he was able to carry out numerous killings until at least 1912. Since police work at the time was not equipped to handle a random serial killer who left the area of the crime immediately afterward, Mueller evaded arrest for over a decade.

DEVILS LAKERS SEE THE SERPENT

Devils Lake, July 0.—Stretched out on the surface of the lake at a point estimated about the middle of the bay of Devils Lake, off Greenwood, the sea serpent last evening basked in the delightful evening atmosphere, while residents of Chautauqua and Greenwood feasted their eyes on the monster that has figured in the legends of Devils lake for nearly a half century.

People who in years past had smiled and jested when the word sea serpent was mentioned, last evening saw it on the waters of Devils lake. Individuals from several different points unknown to each other, saw the serpent between 7:30 and 8 p. m.

There is no mistake about it.

Optical illusions may occur with one or two.

Occasionally one's enthusiasm transfigures objects. But last night the habitant of the island sea was actually, honestly and very distinctly seen. Men whose veracity has never been questioned, and women too, viewed in silent amazement.

E. M. Lewis viewed the monster from the Chautauqua train. He estimated the length between 50 and 60 feet and the body about a foot in diameter. Mr Lewis located it off Greenwood point near the center of the bay. Capt. and Mrs. Walter Furstenau saw it at the same time.

Chas. Pillsbury, not in company of the above, saw the serpent. He estimates the length considerably less However estimating the length of an object a quarter of a mile away, would be precarious at best.

The monster was last seen by Rev. C. L. Wallace, who recently left Devils Lake. It was then in the south end of the lake. The fact that the bridge at the Narrows divides the lake absolutely leads to the conclusion that there are either two serpents in Devils lake or else the frisky old critter vaulted the bridge, which in really is a dam, built of rock, gravel and clay.

In any event the serpent which was known to the Indians years ago, or his off-spring, is still alive and doing nicely, thank you. So far as can be found no one has ever been molested by his serpentship. He tends strictly to his own business and appears just frequently enough to keep alive the stories which promise to go down to posterity.

The Weekly Times-Record of Valley City, North Dakota,
7-22-1915, Page 1.

27

THE TRAIN AND THE SEA SERPENT

JULY 20, 1915
DEVILS LAKE, NORTH DAKOTA

On July 20, 1915, a businessman named E. M. Lewis was a passenger on board a train passing near the shore of Devils Lake, North Dakota, when he saw a sight out his window that he would never forget. It was between fifty and sixty feet long and between a foot and two feet in diameter, as reported in the July 21, 1915 edition of the *Grand Forks Daily Herald*.

Passengers on the train were not the only ones who saw the phenomenon. A number of local residents, from the nearby towns of Chautauqua and Greenwood, saw the creature stretched out on the surface of the bay of Devils Lake, "basking in the delightful evening sunshine shortly before sundown."

Newspaper accounts stated that many residents, standing at multiple vantage points, saw the beast between 7:30 and 8 p.m. "There was no mistake about it," said the reporters. People who had previously scoffed at the stories of a sea serpent in Devils Lake were forced to change their opinions.

An account in the *Weekly Times-Record* of Valley City, North Dakota, said, "Optical illusions may occur with one or two. Occasionally one's enthusiasm transfigures objects. But last night the habitant of the island sea was actually, honestly and very distinctly seen. Men whose veracity has never been questioned, and women too, viewed in silent amazement."

Newspaper accounts listed the identities of specific people who saw the strange apparition either on this occasion or on previous ones, including the train passenger E. M. Lewis; police captain Walter Furstenau, Mrs. Furstenau, Charles Pillsbury, and Reverend C. L. Wallace of the Methodist Episcopal Church. Lewis and Pillsbury were described as "well known businessmen."

The articles mentioned that Reverend Wallace had seen the serpent two years previously, in 1913, on the opposite side of the dike/bridge that divides the lake in half. During the 1915 sighting, it was seen on the west end of the lake. Reporters stated that either it was one beast that somehow "vaulted the bridge," or it was actually two different creatures.

For many decades, the local people had grown up hearing Native American stories about a sea serpent that was living in the lake. They said sightings of the creature had occurred for at least fifty years prior to 1915.

Terror on the Train!

The June 17, 1893 edition of the *Fargo Forum, Daily Republican, and Moorhead Daily News* contained a whimsical story about a party of men in boats who went out onto Devils Lake determined to capture the fabled sea serpent. "The serpent with long, sinuous, shining body and horrid hooded head aloft waited defiantly their approach." Although the veracity of the story is definitely suspect, the article made clear that tales of sea serpents in Devils Lake, North Dakota, were well known long before the 1915 incident.

The *New York Sun*, on August 21, 1894, ran a surprisingly long article that delved into the Devils Lake sea serpent mystery, describing the serpent in great detail as follows: "All descriptions of the serpent agree that it has alligator jaws and glaring red eyes. Its tail is about 80 feet long. The serpent usually appears in August and about sunset. The red glare of the sunset sky is often reflected in the eyes of the serpent like mirrors, and the flashes of red light that go darting here and there as the serpent turns its head, strike terror into the hearts of those on whom they fall. The serpent moves slowly along about half a mile from the shore, and in the course of a day or two makes the round of the lake. At times it lashes the water furiously with its tail and again it leaves a simple, shining wake as it pushes its way along. Sometimes it plays porpoise-fashion, making long and graceful plunges and coming to the surface after long reaches just beneath the surface. The presence of an Indian on the water or near the shore always provokes it into fury. Its color is a slimy green, and it is easy to trace the waves of motion that begin at its head and follow along to its tail, three or four distinct waves being in evidence at the same time. It has ragged and enormous fins on its sides and horny substances that project from its jaws, or directly behind them, and trail along in the water, but which, when it is angered, stick out in a horrible bristling attitude. Its scales sometimes glisten and sometimes lie so close to its back that they seem to be simply an ordinary snake skin. After having made its annual appearance in its journey around the lake, it disappears again for a year."

"The Indians give a most interesting explanation of its presence in the lake, so far from the sea. In some way, they have learned, or it has come down to them in their folklore, that there was once a glacial period on this continent. They assert that this serpent came down with the ice from the great North, and was left to its fate in this lake, and has been there ever since because it could not get away.... The serpent, according to tradition, was caught in the ice and had to move along, or went just ahead of it and became stalled in Devil's Lake, where it has remained ever since to torment the equipoise of the Indians and to interest the whites."

"According to the Indians, the serpent has a most interesting mission to perform. Devil's Lake is brackish and almost salt. The only fishes that live in it are pickerel. It has no outlet, and to account for this mystery, the Indians say there is a subterranean outlet, and the mission of the serpent is to lie on the bottom of the lake and stop that hole up, keeping in the water."

On August 11, 1904, the *Clay Center (Kansas) Times* reported on a sighting of the serpent at Devils Lake: "Devils Lake, N.D. Aug. 6. Campers on the Chautauqua grounds were thrown into consternation tonight by the appearance of what is thought to be a sea serpent in Devil's Lake. Mrs. Edgar La Rue, wife of a newspaperman; Mrs. C. F. Craig, wife of a banker of Leeds, N.D., and Mrs. Carr Cleveland, wife of a prominent businessman of this city, were strolling along the beach when their attention was attracted by a great disturbance in the lake about a mile from the shore. Securing opera glasses, they beheld the head and body of an enormous animal swimming toward the north shore, leaving a trail of foam in its wake."

"Its head was large and snakelike, and apparently of enormous length. Its body appeared thickly covered with large black scales. The women were terrified, and went in search of their husbands. Parties armed with rifles are patrolling the shores but nothing more has been seen of the serpent. A party of Indians later reached town and told of seeing the sea serpent earlier in the day, thus confirming the story of the women."

The women's encounter took place at 5 p.m., and the newspaper accounts about it also stated that "Devils Lake is believed to be bottomless."

Between 1904 and 1915, there were multiple sightings, as evidenced by a story in the July 16, 1914 edition of the *Devils Lake (North Dakota) World* newspaper:

"SEA SERPENT SEEN AGAIN. While out rowing Monday evening near the point south of the Chautauqua grounds, three persons in a boat declare they saw the 'sea serpent' (that has been talked about so much before). While these parties do not care to have their names mentioned in connection with the matter, after three careful investigations, and an interview with these well-known people, we have no hesitation in saying that they saw a very peculiar animal or fish in the lake. When they discovered it, their boat was within ten rods of it and as it raised its head above the water, they had a splendid view and were all able to describe its head as being over two feet long and very broad and with a snout on it something like an alligator, but much wider. The main portion of the body was not exposed to view but the tail was also out of the water and to the best of their judgment the animal was about 20 feet long. The gentleman who was rowing the boat was a well-known doctor and accompanied by two well-known ladies of this community, and they all stated that the commotion in the water caused by the animal swimming was sufficient to capsize a row boat."

"They were afraid the monster would come toward the boat so carefully moved away to a safe distance and watched it swim swiftly away, having its head above water part of the time and at other times it entirely disappeared. As they were near enough to it to see it distinctly there is no question but what they saw a very strange something--whether fish or animal. While we have always laughed at the idea of a 'sea serpent' being seen in the lake, after talking with each of these three people the editor of this paper has become convinced that their story and description is true beyond a doubt."

The various articles about the sea serpent mentioned that investigations would be conducted and search parties would be mounted to seek out the monster. However, there is no record of the monster ever having been found. Nonetheless, it remains one of the more interesting lake monster stories due to the fact that one of the most significant sightings took place on board a train.

28

VAMPIRE EMERGES FROM COLLAPSED RAILROAD TUNNEL

OCTOBER 2, 1925
CHURCH HILL, VIRGINIA

On October 2, 1925, a railroad tunnel collapsed in Church Hill, Virginia, killing four men and burying a locomotive along with ten cars. The tunnel had been built back in 1873 and was already out of commission by 1901. In 1925, it was decided to restore the tunnel, and that's when the collapse happened. About 200 workers managed to survive by crawling under the train cars until they reached the east end of the tunnel and managed to get back to the outside world. As stated before, the final death tally amounted to four men as far as authorities could tell. Rescue efforts only resulted in further collapses, and so the tunnel was sealed off for safety reasons. According to urban legend, one man emerged from the rubble with blood dripping from his mouth and torn flesh hanging from his limbs. This account, true or not, was later conjoined with another area legend called the Richmond Vampire.

The Richmond Vampire had his moniker bestowed upon him after his death, which occurred in 1922, by the way, three years before the tunnel collapse. Buried in the Hollywood Cemetery of Richmond, Virginia, the deceased's name was W.W. Pool, and supposedly the vampire rumor began simply because the W's on the tomb reminded people of fangs. It didn't hurt that Pool's tomb had design aesthetics of the Egyptian Rite of Freemasonry, which only added to the mystique.

In the 1960s, a story came about that Pool was from England and had been run out of his own country for being a vampire. Specifically, it is thought that students cooked up the story at the nearby Virginia Commonwealth University, and by 1976 the tale was published in the *Commonwealth Times*.

The "vampire's tomb" in Hollywood Cemetery.

According to an article by Garry F. Curtis from 1976, "Mr. Pool is an alleged vampire. There seems to be a cult in Richmond that has grown up around him. I find this strange since I've heard that it used to be the 'in' thing among medical students to break in and steal parts of his remains. My informant also claims that W.W. was the inspiration for Barnabas Collins on the old Gothic soap opera *Dark Shadows*. I take this bit of news with a grain of salt, however."

In the mid-1980s, occultists took notice of the legend and began using the mausoleum as a backdrop for their rituals. According to Harry Kollatz Jr. in an article in *Richmond Magazine*, "the iron door of his crypt got jimmied open and fanciful occultists inscribed words and symbols on the outer chamber's walls. Fetishes are still dropped by the gate with some regularity. The glass of the lunette window on the inner wall shattered (presumably from the inside)." [Kollatz Jr., "W.W. Pool: Richmond's Reputed Nosferatu", *Richmond Magazine*.]

Terror on the Train!

In the early 21st Century, someone decided to combine the Richmond Vampire with the Churchill Tunnel collapse. The new story claimed that the blood-drenched, muscular man seen emerging from the tunnel had been feeding on one of the dead. Furthermore, it was the tunnel collapse itself that had somehow awakened this ancient evil. Men chased the ghoulish creature all the way to James River and then into Hollywood Cemetery, where it took refuge in the crypt of W.W. Pool. Some say that as the men rushed into the crypt, the lid of the coffin was closing, while others say the vampire locked itself inside the mausoleum and no one could actually gain ingress.

Undated image of the East Tunnel of Church Hill after the collapse.

Is there any truth to the tale of a badly wounded man emerging from the debris? Possibly. Gregory Maitland of the Virginia Ghosts & Haunting Research Society thinks the wounded man was the muscular Benjamin F. Mosby, who had been shoveling coal into the firebox of the steam locomotive in the tunnel when the collapse occurred. As a result, the boiler ruptured and he was badly burned. It is also said that his teeth were broken during the incident, making them jagged. Poor Mosby didn't live long after he emerged from the tunnel and was later buried in Hollywood Cemetery. That is a logical explanation, as Mosby was, for a fact, a real man who died after emerging badly injured from the tunnel. He also had all the physical characteristics of the alleged vampire, including the muscular physique.

Neither was Pool found to be an English vampire on the run, by the way, and was simply a local accountant for the wealthy Bryan family, owners of the *Richmond Times-Dispatch*. It is thought that he was being frugal when he had his initials placed on the tomb rather than his full name, and the double W's were later interpreted as fangs by excitable college students. As such, the so-called Hollywood Vampire is just as fictitious as anything that ever came out of Tinseltown.

29

FLORIDA'S HAUNTED RAILROAD

DECEMBER 1890
PEMBERTON FERRY, FLORIDA

A s of the writing of this book, the town in Central Florida once known as Pemberton Ferry is now called Croom, and is classified as a ghost town. The railroad arrived in 1884 at Pemberton Ferry, and a few years after its arrival, the strange story you are about to read was first told regarding mysterious happenings there.

In 1890, Pemberton Ferry had a single railroad bridge, which was tended by Job Simmons, a grizzled old railroad veteran. The year before, a terrible accident happened when a train struck a tree that had fallen upon the railroad tracks. The train derailed, and the train engineer was thrown from the cab, falling directly under the engine and being crushed to death.

A few months after this horrific accident, the railroad workers in the area began talking about "weird, strange noises" heard at the particular portion of the track where the previous accident had happened. Since these noises were heard mainly during the "morning run," many of the workers requested that their schedule be changed so that they would not go past the "haunted" section of railroad.

The first incident involving something unexplained happened when the engineer on engine No. 24, while passing Elbow Creek, near where the accident occurred, saw something ominous dead ahead -- a large pine tree lying across the tracks.

Although it was too late to stop the train, the engineer reversed the engine and put on the air brakes. "The huge tree was plainly seen, as he thought, on the track ahead and the engine rushed towards it with headlong speed. It was but a second before they would strike, the engineer thought, and in that brief time was crowded a lifetime. As the engine appeared to strike the tree, he braced himself for the shock and closed his eyes," said the *Buffalo (NY) Weekly Express*, (December 18, 1890 edition).

"To his utter astonishment no shock came, and the engine plunged through what seemed to be the huge tree without hindrance, while a blood-curdling cry came from the track underneath."

Shortly after, the train came to a stop a short distance away, and the train crew walked back to where the engineer and fireman had seen the tree across the tracks. They found nothing. Since only the engineer and fireman had claimed to see the apparition, the other members of the crew disbelieved them and even "laughed" at them.

At that point, the engineer and fireman did not suspect anything supernatural. They thought that perhaps they had been deceived by light and shadows on the track that seemed to be a fallen tree.

But several nights later, they experienced something else on the same section of track that finally convinced them of ghostly happenings. While on a nighttime run, engine No. 24 again saw something frightful on the track a short distance ahead – only this time instead of a fallen tree, it was another train headed at full speed directly toward them. The *Weekly Express* said, "They beheld an engine coming toward them, with lightning speed, not over half a mile away. Her headlight beamed far in advance, while the fire from the fire-box made bright shadows on the pine forests beside."

"Hastily reversing his engine, the engineer whistled for brakes and made ready to jump, but before he could do so, the other engine was upon him, and just as he expected to hear the horrid crash and to feel the shock, the approaching engine disappeared and the track was entirely free."

At the same time, the train crew heard the same blood-curdling cry they had heard before – "a shriek as by someone in great agony," causing the engineer's hair to stand on end, as he heard it.

Stopping the train again, the crew found nothing amiss. But this time, more of the train's crew believed the engineer and the fireman when they said they had seen the oncoming train.

The bizarre incidents along this stretch of railroad continued on almost a weekly basis, being experienced not just by engine No. 24 but also by other train crews.

On December 13, 1890, on engine No. 36, while coming around the curve near the same spot, the engineer saw a tree lying across the track and a man underneath the tree, struggling to get out from under!

"The night was dark, but the bright glare of the head-light made every object as distinct as if at noonday. He reversed his engine with all speed, whistled for brakes and turned on the sand, but his huge engine darted on, hardly unchecked, and the paralyzed engineer imagined death at hand. He stuck to his engine, however, closed his eyes and braced himself for the shock that never came," said the newspaper.

"Instead of striking the tree, the big engine clattered on, groaning and puffing, at the reversed power applied, while as he passed over where he supposed the tree was, loud shrieks filled the air, coming from the track, from the tree-tops, and in all directions. In fact, the engineer said afterward that there seemed to be an internal pandemonium of all the imps set loose at once. As the train stopped, the trainmen hurried out and found the engineer in a half-fainting condition on his engine, while the … fireman was almost dead with fright."

"It was several minutes before they could recover their wits sufficiently to run the train, and when they got to the end of the run the engineer promptly sent in his resignation."

"Several of the railroad men have expressed great incredulity about these reports, and laughed at these men who say they have seen the apparitions and ghosts—that they would like to meet such harmless ghosts, but it is noticed, all the same, that these railroad-men always managed to be absent when a run made at night over this stretch of road. It is the talk of the entire length of the line, and at times it is difficult to get engineers to take the midnight run."

A HAUNTED RAILROAD.

Strange Appearances that are Frightening Servants.

From the St. Louis Globe-Democrat.

Old railroaders, and especially old Job Simmons, who tends the railroad bridge at Pemberton Ferry, Fla., are greatly excited over recent developments regarding a ghost case on the railroad. About a year ago a bad accident occurred near here, where an engineer lost his life, caused by the engine hitting a tree and being thrown from the track. The engineer was thrown from the cab directly under the engine and crushed to death. About three months ago the railroad men of this division began talking of the weird, strange noises heard at one portion of the track on the morning run, and many were so worked up about the matter that they had their runs changed.

The first that was known about the matter is that the engineer on No. 24, while passing Elbow Creek, near where the accident occurred, all of a sudden while looking ahead saw what he thought was a big pine tree lying across the track. The engine was so near that he could not stop, although he reversed the engine and put on the air-brakes. The huge tree was plainly seen, as he thought, on the track ahead, and the engine rushed towards it with headlong speed. It was but a second before they would strike, the engineer thought, and in that brief time was crowded a lifetime. As the engine appeared to strike the tree he braced himself for the shock and closed his eyes.

To his utter astonishment no shock came, and the engine plunged through what seemed to be the huge tree without hindrance, while a blood-curdling cry came from the track underneath. The train came to stop in a short distance, and the train men got out to investigate. Nothing was found, of course, and as it was only the engineer and fireman who had seen this strange appearance, they were laughed at by the other members of the train crew.

Though startled by this occurrence, the engineer and firemen were not convinced of any ghostly apparition until several nights afterward, when, on one moonlight run down on the same section, they beheld an engine coming toward them with lightning speed not over half a mile away. Her headlight beamed far in advance, while the

fire from the fire-box made bright shadows on the pine forests beside. Hastily reversing his engine, the engineer whistled for brakes and made ready to jump, but before he could do so the other engine was upon him, and just as he expected to hear the horrid crash and to feel the shock, the approaching engine disappeared and the track was entirely free. This apparition was accompanied by the same blood-curdling cry, a shriek as by some one in great agony, and the engineer says that his hair fairly stood on end as he heard it. Again the train stopped, but as one or two of the trainmen had seen the same occurrence, more of them believed the engineer's story. After this it got to be almost a weekly thing for one or more of the train crew to have experience of this kind.

Last Saturday on engine No. 36, while coming around the curve near this spot, the engineer, who is a new hand, by the way, discerned a tree lying across the track, as he thought, while underneath it was revealed the struggling figure of a man held prostrate by the limbs. The night was dark, but the bright glare of the head-light made every object as distinct as if at noonday. He reversed his engine with all speed, whistled for brakes and turned on the sand, but his huge engine darted on, hardly unchecked, and the paralyzed engineer imagined death at hand. He stuck to his engine, however, closed his eyes and braced himself for the shock that never came. Instead of striking the tree, the big engine clattered on, groaning and puffing, at the reversal power applied, while as he passed over where he supposed the tree was, loud shrieks filled the air, coming from the track, from the tree-tops, and in all directions. In fact, the engineer said afterward that there seemed to be an infernal pandemonium of all the imps set loose at once. As the train stopped the trainmen hurried out and found the engineer in a half-fainting condition on his engine, while the colored fireman was almost dead with fright. It was several minutes before they could recover their wits sufficiently to run the train, and when they got to the end of the run the engineer promptly sent in his resignation.

Several of the railroad-men have expressed great incredulity about these reports, and laughed at these men who say they have seen the apparitions and ghosts—that they would like to meet such harmless ghosts, but it is noticed, all the same, that these railroad-men always managed to be absent when a run is made at night over this stretch of road. It is the talk of the entire length of the line, and at times it is difficult to get engineers to take the midnight run.

Buffalo (NY) Weekly Express, 12-18-1890, p. 5.

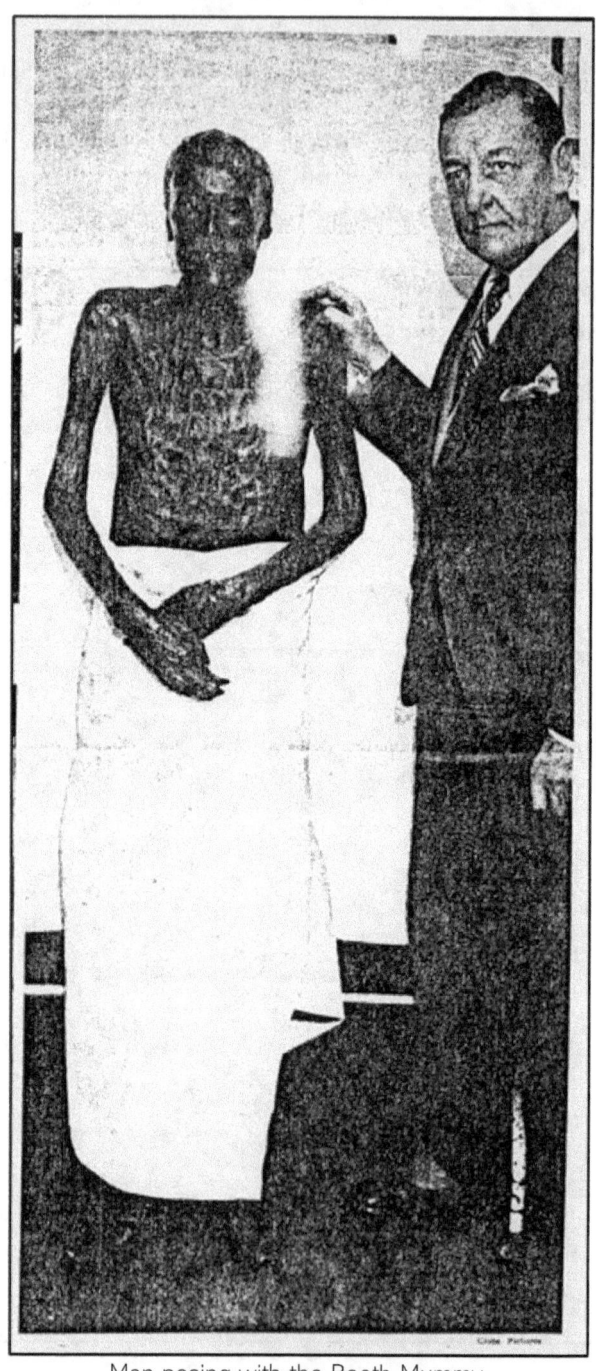

Man posing with the Booth Mummy.

30

CURSED MUMMY CAUSES TRAIN CRASH

1920
NEAR SAN DIEGO, CALIFORNIA

Since we began our journey into the haunted realm of ghostly trains with Lincoln's phantom funeral train, we thought it might be appropriate to close this book with the tale of John Wilkes Booth's cursed mummy causing a train crash. Of course, a story as wild as that entails some context before we can get to the train crash. One of the first important things to note is that the cursed mummy, which did for a fact exist, may not have been John Wilkes Booth.

History tells us that on April 14, 1865, an actor named John Wilkes Booth assassinated Abraham Lincoln during a play at Ford's Theater. Though General Robert E. Lee had surrendered and the Civil War was basically over, General Joseph E. Johnston was still fighting against the Union. In Booth's mind, the war wasn't over yet, and he and his other co-conspirators believed that killing Lincoln could aid the Confederacy. And so Booth carried out his terrible deed. In that regard, history is quite clear. Where history becomes uncertain is in regard to the details of Booth's death. According to accepted history, Booth fled on horseback towards Southern Maryland. Twelve days later, he was found within a barn on a farm in rural Northern Virginia. There he was shot through the neck and killed.

Full view of the Booth Mummy.

However, much like Western outlaws Butch Cassidy, Billy the Kid, and Jesse James, there are stories that the wrong man was killed and Booth lived on. Theories abound as to why this happened, with some alleging that it was a government-endorsed conspiracy to fake Booth's death—either out of shame for not being able to apprehend him or because the government had, in fact, condoned the assassination. Whatever the case, Booth supposedly took on the alias of John St. Helen and moved to Texas, at first settling near Glen Rose before moving to Granbury, where he worked as a bartender.

Terror on the Train!

In 1877 in Granbury, St. Helen mistakenly believed that he was dying. On his "death bed," St. Helen confessed to a young lawyer he had worked with in the past, Finis L. Bates, that he was, in fact, John Wilkes Booth. However, St. Helen pulled through and didn't die. Before fleeing Granbury, he explained to Bates that it was President Johnson himself who had authorized Lincoln's assassination. Johnson had even given Booth a special password allowing him to escape from authorities in on the plot. The man shot in the barn was just a random fugitive who was later passed off as Booth so that the real presidential assassin could slip away.

Vintage postcard of Granbury, Texas.

Many years after his disappearance from Granbury, Booth/St. Helen resurfaced in the newspapers under the alias of David E. George. Bates just happened to read about the death of George, who committed suicide in Enid, Oklahoma, on January 13, 1903. What caught Bates's eye, naturally, was the detail that George claimed to be John Wilkes Booth!

According to the article, George had attempted suicide nine months earlier when he again thought he was dying. George confessed to the wife of a local Methodist preacher that "I am not David Elihu George. I am the one who killed the best man that ever lived. I am J. Wilkes Booth." Though the suicide attempt nine months earlier in 1902 had failed, George's second attempt did not. George had ingested a lethal amount of arsenic, which in turn also mummified his body.

David E. George shortly after his death.

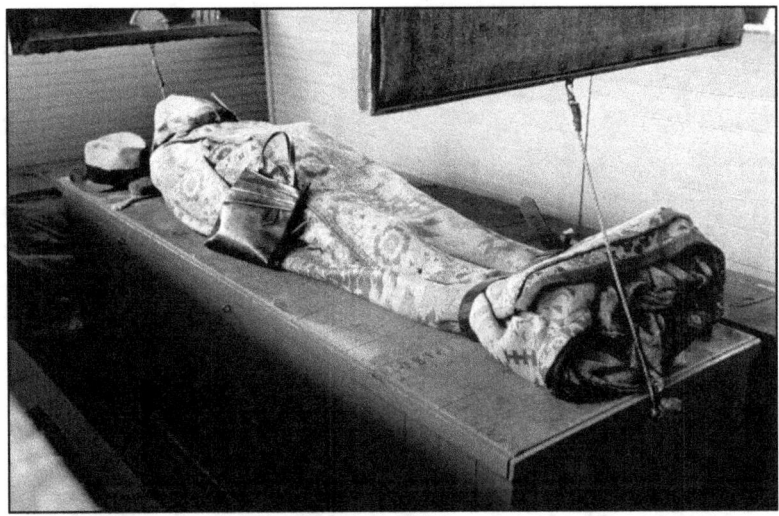

The mummy under wraps.

Bates rushed to Enid upon reading the article in hopes of procuring Booth's mummified body. When he arrived, the body had further mummified thanks to the embalming fluid used by W.B. Penniman at his mortuary/furniture shop. However, Penniman himself wanted to use the unclaimed body as an attraction for his shop and refused to let Bates claim it. For several years, Booth's mummified corpse, now with glass eyes, sat upon the porch reading a newspaper. Bates found another way to exploit the wild story by writing a book, *Escape and Suicide of John Wilkes Booth: Written for the Correction of History*, in 1907. Around that same time, Bates did manage to finally procure the corpse itself. He did so with the help of an Oklahoma judge, who thought that Bates would actually bury the body since it was a former client of his. Instead, Bates rented out the notorious mummy to state fairs and carnivals. In his article on the mummy for *History.com*, Christopher Klein put it best when he wrote that the mummy "became a freak-show mirror image to the solemn funeral train procession taken by Lincoln's embalmed body in the weeks after the assassination." [Klein, "The John Wilkes Booth Mummy That Toured America," *History.com* (April 17, 2015). *https://www.history.com/news/the-john-wilkes-booth-mummy-that-toured-america*]

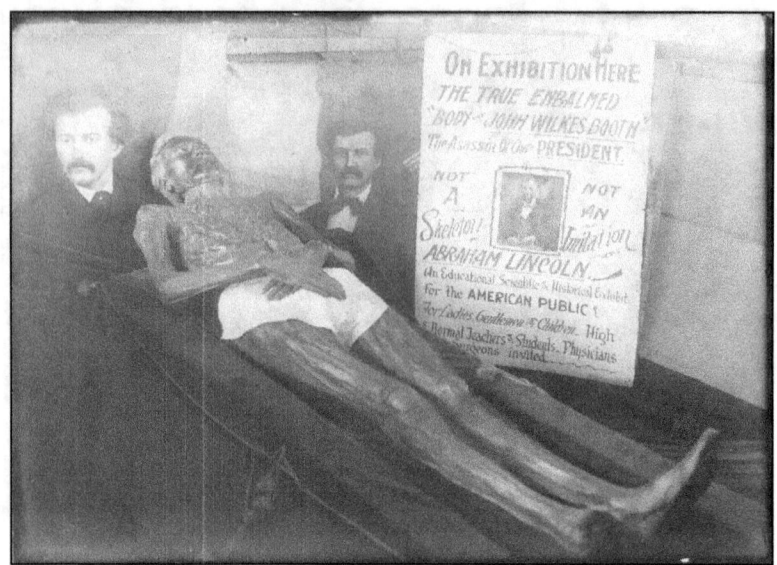

The mummy on display.

And like any good mummy, this one was cursed. The first inclination of the Booth Mummy's curse came when a circus train transporting the body crashed on its way to San Diego in 1920. Eight people died along with many of the so-called "freak show" animals on the train.

In Gordon Grice's article, "The Mummy of John Wilkes Booth," for This Land Press in 2016, the author wrote, "The corpse traveled as part of a show featuring lavish live marriages and freak animals. It emerged unscathed from a train wreck that killed eight people, which may have been when it picked up the legend of a Tut-style curse. Tutankhamen had only recently been dug up, and such stories were in vogue."

Unfortunately, none of the articles on Booth and the train crash cite an exact date or a source. While you'd think a circus train wreck would be big news, and thus easy to find, mention of the crash was hard to find in newspapers. *The Independent* of December 20, 1920, was the only record that seemed to match in terms of location. It stated the following: "SAN DIEGO, December 20—A broken rail caused the train carrying the Wortham shows to leave the track, it was reported here. Three employees were injured, one seriously, it was reported here. The train arrived here later."

Terror on the Train!

The Independent of December 20, 1920.

The little blurb was clearly nothing dramatic other than the serious injury of one of the employees. Was it a separate incident entirely, or did the story get blown out of proportion? The *Columbus Weekly Advocate* of July 15, 1920 called the Wortham Shows the biggest carnival company in the United States. The traveling circus entailed a 35-car train carrying four hundred people in all. In terms of animals, it was said to carry "fifty wild animals" and "one hundred monkeys." No mention was made of any mummies. But still, if the Booth Mummy managed to derail the train of the Wortham Circus, that would be quite a feat.

Two other train wrecks where precisely eight people died were found in newspapers from 1920, but none of them mentioned the train being San Diego-bound nor having circus animals on board. On the note of circus train crashes, a big one occurred two years prior in 1918 in the form of the Hammond circus train wreck of June 22, 1918—one of the worst train wrecks in U.S. history. Eighty-six people were killed and 127 more were injured. Though the Booth Mummy may not have been on the train, one of his future owners, John Harkin, at the time the most famous "tattooed man" in the circus business, was. He bought the mummy in 1932, and it eventually ruined Harkin financially as well.

As for the mummy's original owner, Bates himself died not long after, and some like to claim it was due to the ridicule he suffered from writing the book. The so-called Carnival King of the Southwest, William Evans, purchased the mummy from Bates's widow and began exhibiting it across the country as Bates had done. The mummy eventually led to his financial ruin and Evans died when he was shot in a Chicago holdup in 1933.

173

Under new ownership, the Booth Mummy continued touring the country well into the 1950s. Its history throughout the 1960s is sketchy—presumably it was mothballed for a time—and all we know is that the mummy was last seen sometime in the 1970s. Though the exact date of the last showing is never given in any sources, I did find reports that in 1977, an optometrist in Barberton, Ohio, claimed his family was in possession of the mummy. That same year, the *Sedalia Democrat* reported that the FBI was examining 18 missing pages recently found from Booth's old diary. Supposedly, these missing pages revealed much, such as that Booth claimed he was working for the secretary of war when he killed Lincoln.

Today the mummy is still missing, with reports stating that it's in the hands of a private collector somewhere.

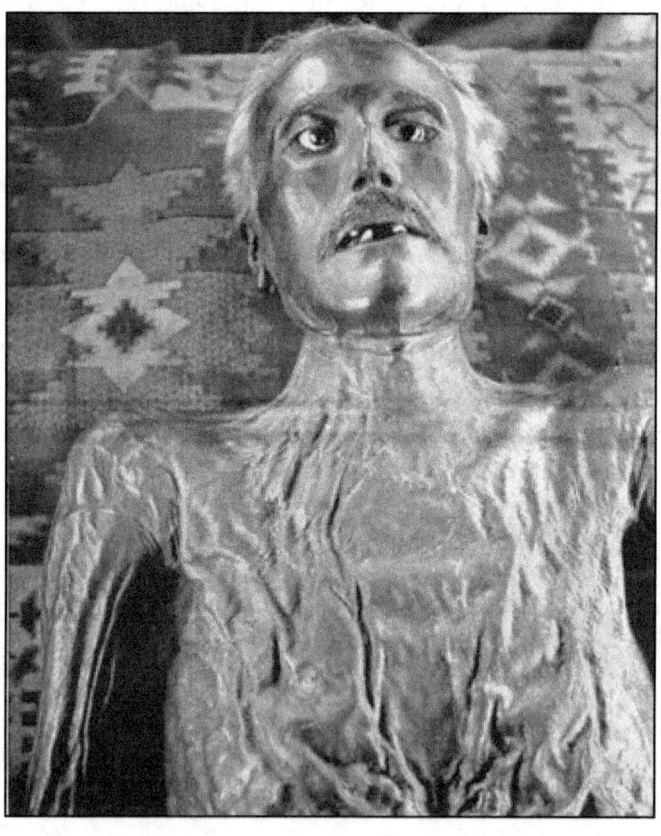

BIBLIOGRAPHY

Books

Clark, Jerome. *Unnatural Phenomena: A Guide to the Bizarre Wonders of North America*. Santa Barbara, CA: ABC-CLIO, 2005.

Johnston, Alva. "'JOHN WILKES BOOTH' ON TOUR." *Saturday Evening Post* (February 10, 1938).
http://www.granburydepot.org/z/biog/BoothJohnWilkesOnTour.htm

Klein, Christopher. "The John Wilkes Booth Mummy That Toured America." History.com (April 17, 2015)
https://www.history.com/news/the-john-wilkes-booth-mummy-that-toured-america

Kollatz Jr., Harry. "W.W. Pool: Richmond's Reputed Nosferatu." *Richmond Magazine* (October 30, 2013).
https://richmondmagazine.com/arts-entertainment/richmonds-reputed-nosferatu/

Murray, Earl. *Ghosts of the Old West*. Dorset Press, 1988.

INDEX

ABOUT NOE TORRES

Noe Torres is a recognized expert in the field of UFOs and the paranormal. He is an author, publisher, and member of the Mutual UFO Network (MUFON). He holds a Bachelor's in English and a Master's in Library Science from the University of Texas at Austin. He has written one of the most popular books about the famous Roswell Incident, titled *Ultimate Guide to the Roswell UFO Crash*, which is the top selling book among tourists visiting Roswell, New Mexico. He has also written several other well-reviewed books, including *Mexico's Roswell, The Other Roswell, Aliens in the Forest, Fallen Angel*, and *The Coyame Incident*.

Noe has appeared on several nationally-broadcast television shows, including season 2, episode 1 of the Travel Channel's *Mysteries of the Outdoors*, titled "Strange Attraction," which premiered in August 2017. In that show, he is interviewed extensively about unexplained mysteries in Big Bend National Park. Also, in 2017, Noe was featured in an episode titled "The Marfa Lights" for the TV series *Mysteries of the Unexplained*. In 2008, he appeared in season 1, episode 4 of the History Channel's *UFO Hunters*, in a show called "Crash and Retrieval."

Noe has appeared several times on George Noory's famous radio show *Coast to Coast AM*, as well as on The Jeff Rense Program and may other shows. He is also in high demand as a speaker at UFO and paranormal conferences and festivals, having been a featured speaker at the 2017 International UFO Congress in Scottsdale, Arizona. He has also spoken five times at the annual Roswell UFO Conference and at many other UFO conferences throughout the United States and Mexico.

ABOUT JOHN LEMAY

John LeMay was born and raised in Roswell, NM, the "UFO Capital of the World." He is the author of over 50 books, many of them on the history of the Southwest such as *Tall Tales and Half Truths of Billy the Kid*, and *Roswell USA: Towns That Celebrate UFOs, Lake Monsters, Bigfoot and Other Weirdness*. In addition to non-fiction, he is also the author of the novels *The Noted Desperado Pancho Dumez* and *Once Upon a Time in Fort Sumner*. He is also the editor/publisher of *Strange West Magazine* and has written for Western journals and magazines such as *True West*, *The Coalition Journal*, the *Tombstone Epitaph*, and the *Wild West History Association Journal*. He is a Past President of the Board of Directors for the Historical Society for Southeast New Mexico.

The following titles are available for purchase on Amazon.com, and are available to bookstores at a wholesale discount via Ingram Content Group (ISBNs of available editions listed for this purpose)

CRYPTOZOOLOGY/COWBOYS & SAURIANS

Cowboys & Saurians: Prehistoric Beasts as Seen by the Pioneers explores dinosaur sightings from the pioneer period via real newspaper reports from the time. Well-known cases like the Tombstone Thunderbird are covered along with more obscure cases like the Crosswicks Monster and more. Softcover (357 pp/5.06" X 7.8") Suggested Retail: $19.95 ISBN: 978-1-7341546-1-0

Cowboys & Saurians: Ice Age zeroes in on snowbound saurians like the Ceratosaurus of the Arctic Circle and a Tyrannosaurus of the Tundra, as well as sightings of Ice Age megafauna like mammoths, glyptodonts, Sarkastodons and Sabertoothed tigers. Tales of a land that time forgot in the Arctic are also covered. Softcover (264 pp/5.06" X 7.8") Suggested Retail: $14.99 ISBN: 978-1-7341546-7-2

Southerners & Saurians takes the series formula of exploring newspaper accounts of monsters in the pioneer period with an eye to the Old South. In addition to dinosaurs are covered Lizardmen, Frogmen, giant leeches and mosquitoes, and the Dingocroc, which might be an alien rather than a prehistoric survivor. Softcover (202 pp/5.06" X 7.8") Suggested Retail: $13.99 ISBN: 978-1-7344730-4-9

Cowboys & Saurians South of the Border explores the saurians of Central and South America, like the Patagonian Plesiosaurus that was really an Iemisch, plus tales of the Neo-Mylodon, a menacing monster from underground called the Minhocao, Glyptodonts, and even Bolivia's three-headed dinosaur! Softcover (412 pp/5.06"X7.8") Suggested Retail: $17.95 ISBN: 978-1-953221-73-5

UFOLOGY/THE REAL COWBOYS & ALIENS IN CONJUNCTION WITH ROSWELL BOOKS

The Real Cowboys and Aliens: Early American UFOs explores UFO sightings in the USA between the years 1800-1864. Stories of encounters sometimes involved famous figures in U.S. history such as Lewis and Clark, and Thomas Jefferson.Hardcover (242pp/6" X 9") Softcover (262 pp/5.06" 7.8") Suggested Retail: $24.99 (hc)/$15.95(sc) ISBN: 978-1-7341546-8-9\(hc)/978-1-7344 730-8-7(sc)

The second entry in the series, *Old West UFOs*, covers reports spanning the years 1865-1895. Includes tales of Men in Black, Reptilians, Spring-Heeled Jack, Sasquatch from space, and other alien beings, in addition to the UFOs and airships. Hardcover (276 pp/6" X 9") Softcover (308 pp/5.06" X 7.8") Suggested Retail: $29.95 (hc)/$17.95(sc) ISBN: 978-1-7344730-0-1 (hc)/ 978-1-73447 30-2-5 (sc)

The third entry in the series, *The Coming of the Airships*, encompasses a short time frame with an incredibly high concentration of airship sightings between 1896-1899. The famous Aurora, Texas, UFO crash of 1897 is covered in depth along with many others. Hardcover (196 pp/6" X 9") Softcover (222 pp/5.06" X 7.8") Suggested Retail: $24.99 (hc)/$15.95(sc) ISBN: 978-1-7347816 -1-8 (hc)/978-1-7347816-0-1(sc)

Featuring cases the authors missed, *The Lost Cases* covers things such as the skyquakes recorded by Lewis and Clark, airships and the Spanish American War, Pancho Villa and crystal skulls, lost alien tribe of the Tundra, invisible alien monsters, the Great Moon Hoax of 1835, hellhounds and airships, the Sonora Airship Club and more. Softcover (252 pp/5.06" X 7.8") Suggested Retail: $18.99 ISBN: 978-1-953221-55-1

Cowboys & Saurians: Dinosaurs Down Under takes the series to Australia to explore tales of the cattle devouring Burrunjor, the dreaded Diprotodon, the terrible Tantanoola Tiger, the marsupial Sasquatch known as the Yowie, plus Thylacines, Bunyips, giant rabbits, Megalodons and dinosaurs in nearby New Zealand. Softcover (240 pp/ 5.06" X 7.8") Suggested Retail: $14.95 ISBN: 978-1-953221-34-6

As the title suggest, *Cowboys & Saurians in the Modern Era* takes the series into the 20th Century with tales of the Texas Pterosaur flap of 1976, the Bladenboro Beast of the 1950s, the Busco Turtle Beast of the 1940s, dinosaur sightings in the Great Depression and far out tales of mini-mastodons, dinosaur men, and Snallygasters. Softcover (320 pp/ 5.06" X 7.8") Suggested Retail: $19.95 ISBN: 978-1-953221-22-3

Settlers & Serpents wrangles the best "Snaik Stories" of the Southwest and beyond in a single volume. Whether it's simple giant snakes or lake serpents, they're corralled in the pages within. Also included are entries on the Leviathan in Mesoamerica and the Southwest plus a detailed look at the giant rattlesnake of Pecos Pueblo. Softcover (180 pp/ 5.06" X 7.8") Suggested Retail: $14.99 ISBN: 978-1-953221-21-6

Written for young readers ages 9-12, *Monsters of the Old South* collects the best creature stories of the White River Monster, Green Eyes, the Crocodingo, the Averasboro Gallinipper, the Tennessee Snake Woman, the Arkansas Gowrow, Bigfoot in the Mississippi River and more. Softcover (122 pp/4.25" X 7") Suggested Retail: $12.99 ISBN: 978-17347816-9-4

Early 20th Century UFOs kicks off a new series that investigates UFO sightings of the early 1900s. Includes tales of UFOs sighted over the *Titanic* as it sunk, Nikola Tesla receiving messages from the stars, an alien being found encased in ice, and a possible virus from outer space!Hardcover (196 pp/6" X 9") Softcover (222 pp/5.06" X 7.8") Suggested Retail: $27.99 (hc)/$16.95(sc) ISBN: 978-1-7347816-1-8 (hc)/978-1-73478 16-0-1(sc)

UFOs in the Roaring Twenties takes a look at UFO sightings in the 1920s just as the title suggests, along with accounts of Mothman in Nebraska, Lincoln LaPaz's first UFO case, Men in Black investigating an airship crash in Braxton County, West Virginia, Camden's Cosmic Sniper, and much more! Softcover (248 pp/5.06" X 7.8") Suggested Retail: $19.99 ISBN: 978-1-953221-51-3

UFOs of the Turbulent Thirties concludes the authors' investigation of the last unexplored decade of Ufology in the Great Depression with accounts of Mothman, Ghost Fliers, Nazi Bells, the Underground City of the Lizard People, a vanished village on the tundra, and even gangsters and aliens. Softcover (212 pp/5.06" X 7.8") Suggested Retail: $17.95 ISBN: 978-1-953221-35-3

Written for young readers ages 9-12, *Space Monsters of the Old West* collects the best alien sightings of the Wild West including Mummies from Mars, Bigfoot from the Moon, Pascagoula's space ghouls, the Crawfordsville Monster, Spring-Heeled Jack, Blobs from space, and even the dinosaurian alien creatures that invaded Van Meter, Iowa. Softcover (120 pp/4.25" X 7") Suggested Retail: $12.99 ISBN: 978-1-953221-87-2

COWBOYS & MONSTERS

Cowboys & Monsters features potentially true stories of real vampires, werewolves, and even mummies unique to America's Wild West period. Examples include the cursed mummy of John Wilkes Booth, New Orleans immortal vampire Jacques St. Germain, precursors to the Beast of Bray Road, and the origins of Skinwalker Ranch. Softcover (316 pp/5.06" X 7.8") Suggested Retail: $19.99 ISBN: 978-1-953221-46-9

The first entry in this trilogy of non-fiction terror sinks its teeth into the lore of the vampire in North America and Mexico, with detailed rundowns on the vampire hunters of Exeter, Rhode Island, a tribe of Bat People, the nocturnal shape-shifting vampire witches of Tlaxcala, the immortal ways of Comte St. Germain in New Orleans and more. Softcover (200 pp/ 5.06" X 7.8") Suggested Retail: $12.99 ISBN: 978-1-953221-38-4

Mummies of the Americas explores Death Valley's city of the Dead, King Tut's Tomb along the Arkansas, the Egyptian City of the Grand Canyon plus the famous mummies of John Wilkes Boothe, Elmer McCurdy, the Cardiff Giant, the Mummy of Helldorado, and even Billy the Kid's pickled trigger finger! Softcover (200 pp/5.06" X 7.8") Suggested Retail: $12.99 ISBN: 978-1-953221-37-7

Cowboys & Dogmen is devoted to tales of werewolves of the Wild West including the dreaded Navajo skinwalker, the Watrous Werewolf, the Beast of the Land Between Lakes, the Hellhounds of El Dorado Canyon, the dreaded Dog Eater, the Wahhoo, the Wolf Man of Versailles, the Michigan Dog-Man and more! Softcover (212 pp/5.06" X 7.8") Suggested Retail: $12.99 ISBN: 978-1-953221-36-0

FICTION/ MISC. HISTORY

The first novel from historian John LeMay weaves a fantastic web of fiction via real life mysteries and legends of New Mexico, namely the puzzling theft and return of Billy the Kid's tombstone in 1976, the legend of the Lost Adams Diggings, the villainous Santa Fe Ring, and the enigmatic Acoma Mesa. Softcover (250 pp/5.5" X 7.5") Suggested Retail: $14.95 ISBN: 978-1-953221-42-1

The year is 1950, and old timers connected to the long-dead outlaw Billy the Kid are turning up murdered in New Mexico. Some blame the killings on the avenging witch of the Navajo nation, the skinwalker, while others think it's no coincidence that a man claiming to be a surviving Billy the Kid is set to meet with the governor soon... Softcover (260 pp/5.5" X 7.5") Suggested Retail: $16.95 ISBN: 978-1-953221-32-2

Roswell, USA, the long-forgotten debut work of John LeMay, is available again and covers the minutia of the infamous Roswell UFO Crash of 1947. Notable chapters include tales of an alien ghost haunting the old airbase, monsters in the nearby Bottomless Lakes, and even a dinosaur sighting outside of town. Softcover (248 pp/6" X 9") Suggested Retail: $14.95 ISBN: 978-0-9817597-5-3

This biography, for the first time ever, tells the history of western journalist Ash Upson, who ghostwrote Pat Garrett's The Authentic Life of Billy the Kid in 1882 and also reproduces many of Upson's letters that detailed the harsh realities of frontier life in New Mexico during the turbulent Lincoln County War. Softcover (318 pp/5.5" X 8.5") Suggested Retail: $16.99 ISBN: 978-1953221919

LEGEND & LORE OF THE LOST ADAMS

JOHN LEMAY

LA LLORONA

Her Kith & Kin

JOHN LEMAY

Tales of terror from the Southwest!

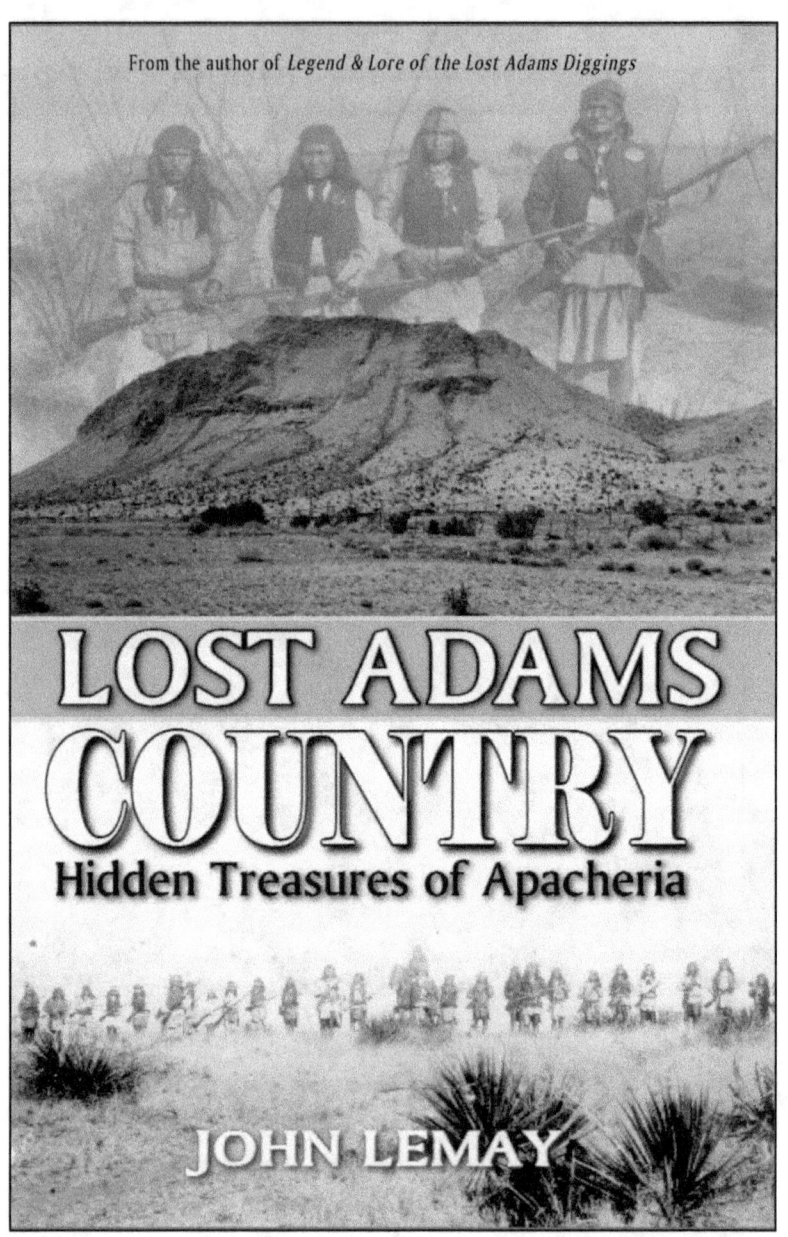

From the author of *Legend & Lore of the Lost Adams Diggings*

LOST ADAMS
COUNTRY
Hidden Treasures of Apacheria

JOHN LEMAY